AUTHORITY CONTENT

THE SIMPLE SYSTEM FOR BUILDING
YOUR BRAND, SALES, & CREDIBILITY

By David Jenyns

Cataloguing-in-Publication entry is available from the National Library of Australia

ISBN: 978-0-646-95564-3 (paperback)

To book David for a speaking engagement, get in touch or become a stockist, contact:

Web: www.AuthorityContent.com
Email: info@melbourneSEOservices.com
Phone: 1300 662 979
Address: 51 McLeod Rd, Mount Martha, Victoria, Australia 3934

First edition.
Cover Design: Igor Vasic
Interior Design: Susan Cooper

A special thanks to...

Carrolyn, Nathaniel, Elaine, Melissa, Sally, Adrian, Mark, Adam, Timbo, Steve, Mike, Troy, Pete, Jen, Nik, Andrew, Brent, Dale, Ed, Greg, Nic, Stuart, Emma, Warrick, Brad, Antony, Cosi, Helen, Brian, Ari, Conrad, Rand, Jen, Mark, Yanik, Steve, Rakhal, Darren, Ken, Yaro, Gideon, Leslie, Nick, James, Luke, Erik, Jake, Adam, Anthony, John, Dorothy, Damien, Evan, Anne, Ken, Scott, Nick, Leslie, Anthony, Ben, Evan, Eric, Dori, Jake, Damien, Dan, Conrad, David, Declan, Charles, Keith, Erik, James, Eugene, Kylie, Laura, Shane, Samuel, Sasha, Raul, Nathan, Jeff, Mark, Jonathan, Donal, Perry, Brendon, Russell, Tim, Louise, the Melbourne SEO & Video team and our awesome clients.

What have people been saying about Authority Content?

If you are looking to build your expert positioning within your industry, 'Authority Content' will show you the way. One of the best marketing books I've read in a very long time. *Joe Vitale, author of The Awakened Millionaire and Hypnotic Writing*

As Tony Robbins says, "Ask a better question and you'll get a better answer." Authority Content forces you to ask the important, difficult questions about your content marketing strategy, and because of this, it helps you get to the core of how to accomplish what you really want with your marketing. *Stephan Spencer, co-author of The Art of SEO, co-author of Social eCommerce and author of Google Power Search*

I spent years thinking I had a good marketing strategy until Dave taught me the Authority Content model. It has catapulted me into "Authority" status and the growth of my business has followed suit. This is a game changer and comes with actual practical things to do, rather than just a whole lot of bloated theory. *Troy Dean, founder of WP Elevation*

David Jenyns really is the authority on content - and this book proves it. Smart, totally relevant and immeasurably practical, 'Authority Content' is a book of great value. *Andrew Griffiths, Australia's #1 Small Business Author*

In an ever increasing noisy world of marketing promotions and content it is only becoming more and more difficult to get your brand seen and heard by potential clients and customers. In this

book Dave will show you the secret weapon on how to actually cut through all the noise and CRUSH it in business. I've seen him do it time and time again, and there is a strong reason everyone knows him as the go-to SEO guy. One word. AUTHORITY.
Nathan Chan, publisher of Foundr Magazine

Despite the ever changing nature of online marketing, the constructs found in 'Authority Content' will stand the test of time. David Jenyns wisely takes a holistic approach to marketing rather than chasing the latest shiny object.
Erik Qualman, #1 Bestselling & Pulitzer Prize Nominated Author

I whole heartedly believe in the principles of this book. It has taken me from zero to a multiple seven figure business. Now it's your turn to discover how to use 'Authority Content' to transform your business and personal success.
Dale Beaumont, founder & CEO of Business Blueprint

Powerful info for business owners looking for a strategic marketing advantage without a big budget. Helps you gain and maintain attention, engagement and trust.
Jonathan Mizel, founder of Email Traffic Academy

If you are trying to market a business online without being an authority in your niche, you're just wasting your time. In this quick, but information packed read, David explains his approach to creating authority, why it works, and the simple action steps any business owner can take right now to make it happen. His definition of "Authority Content" (see page 19) is very much what we teach as well and his story-based presentation style makes for an easy and enjoyable read. For the newcomer or anyone struggling

with marketing, this book is a must read, but even if you are already doing Content Marketing or Inbound Marketing, the couple of hours it will take to read this book is well worth your time.
Leslie Rohde, co-founder of The Marketer's Braintrust

Dave has built a fantastic system to help almost anyone in any industry rise above the masses & get attention... possibly the greatest commodity in today's busy world. Dave's a deep-thinker, a fanatical implementer & a great friend. Read this book. It will change how you look at your brand & your business.
Mike Rhodes, founder of WebSavvy, PPCsavvy & AgencySavvy

There's never been a better time to market your business. 'Authority Content' is living proof of that. Read it. Do it.
Tim Reid, host of The Small Business Big Marketing Show

Content has always been the best form of marketing. Jay Abraham called it 'preselling' well before the advent of the internet. Jenyns has defined it for a new generation of business owners, as a driver of web-traffic, as a tool to capture leads, as a mechanism for delivering exceptional customer service.
James Tuckerman, publisher of Anthill Magazine

Every single marketing effort I've made in the last 5 years has been to achieve one thing, authority. Using content marketing, I've managed to do that and launch a string of successful companies from online services, to memberships to local bricks and mortar businesses. There's always been a lot of noise in the SEO world, but as Dave Jenyns points out in 'Authority Content', focusing on producing quality content and building authority is one that never gets old. If you want to build your authority, your trust, reputation

and your Google Rankings, 'Authority Content' is where it's at.
Dan Norris, co-founder WP Curve

I've known and watched David's work for years and can confirm, he's better than the real deal and someone "I" follow and have learned a ton from through the years! 'Authority Content' is extremely well thought out, proven and perhaps his best work. You're going to love it.
Dori Friend, founder SEO Nitro

One of the most refreshing marketing books I've read in a long time. Clear, concise, actionable and useful for anyone who markets online.
Bart Baggett, author of Success Secrets of the Rich and Happy.

The web changes all the time. The trick is to know where it's heading and be positioned ahead of the curve. David Jenyns has done exactly that with 'Authority Content'. This is modern SEO at it's very finest. It changes the way you think and behave about content and search. It's a must read for any digital marketer or business owner marketing online.
Greg Cassar, CEO of Collective.com.au

David Jenyns has long been one of my go-to contacts for advice on content marketing, especially anything to do with video and search engine optimisation. I was so pleased to see he has taken his knowledge and experience helping clients and created this ground-breaking book on Authority Content. If you're looking to attract customers to your online business and become a leading authority online, this is a must-read.
Yaro Starak, founder of Entrepreneurs-Journey.com

David Jenyns is one sharp marketer. Do yourself a favour, read this book from cover to cover and take massive action - you'll thank me later!
Adam Houlihan, author of Social Media Secret Sauce & The LinkedIn Playbook.

I know authority content works because I've seen it first hand. David runs a smooth operation from recording workshops, to turning them into products, to sharing the content around the web. This isn't a theoretical book - 'Authority Content' is a proven recipe for building maximum trust in minimum time. Every business owner should be applying this system.
Chris Mosely founder of The Cluster Co Working Space

'Authority Content' is not a book about content or authority! Finally, a book with a systemic step-by-step process about how to establish your reputation and trust with your market. Remember, your authority follows a power law... a very small select group get all of the spoils of reputation. Use this book to dramatically increase your odds of being in this small group.
Nikesh Thakorlal, founder of ArchitectureOfPersuasion.com

CONTENTS

INTRODUCTION

Most marketing and business related books don't age well.

There's the occasional exception though, such as "Ogilvy on Advertising", which is a classic. But for the most part, books that teach any kind of marketing or advertising tactics tend to have a relatively short shelf life.

The reason is that technology, culture and life move fast. An effective tactic today can and will (more often than not), be totally ineffectual in a remarkably short period of time.

This small window of opportunity matters to me and it should matter to you. There's an "expiry date" on a lot of the material you read and, unless quickly implemented, you won't even move the needle on your business's bottom line.

In saying that, there's nothing wrong with writing a book that's relevant for a couple of years before disappearing into obscurity. You can still help a lot of people that way, but that short-term thinking has never been my style.

Looking back at the businesses I've built over the past 15 years, I've demonstrated a consistent approach to developing and teaching strategies that are capable of withstanding the test of time. I figure that if I'm going to do something, I might as well make it evergreen.

So, when I sat down to write this book, I asked myself, "What would it take to write a marketing book that will still be just as relevant in five or ten years' time as it is today?"

The core marketing strategy that I employ today has evolved to stay in line with the maturing of the Internet and has been gradually refined to become even more effective. But it's still based on the same principles that I discovered (almost accidentally) and found to be effective so many years ago.

I say "accidentally", not because I was randomly putting things online until something finally worked, but because the system I first created just seemed to be the sensible way to grow my business and spread the word about our products and services. I eventually dubbed this system "Authority Content". It's only looking back at that coincidence now that I can say "Wow! The implementation of this method was really the turning point for my business and my marketing abilities."

While other marketers, especially those in the Search Engine Optimisation (SEO) space, had to keep on totally overhauling their approach to cope with changes in the marketplace, my system never seemed to need more than the occasional tweak to keep powering forward.

If anything, Authority Content has become more effective over time. In short, it's a powerful marketing strategy that establishes you and your business as the authority in your industry – systematically and predictably.

So, with that knowledge, why couldn't I write a book that can withstand the test of time too?

That's what I want for you and your business. I want to provide you with a marketing strategy that will serve you today, tomorrow and for years to come. Having to constantly alter your approach every time the 'wind changes' is expensive and wearisome. By the time you've finished reading this book, you will have a marketing strategy that you can tailor to your specific business and industry – and it will work for a lifetime.

I can say this, because I've proven it to be hugely profitable for our clients, my students and myself. And I believe Authority Content will work for you too.

Be sure to take the time to absorb this information properly. Much of the second half of this book describes the practical steps I recommend, but resist the temptation to skip over the first half and dive straight into the tactics. It's crucial you understand exactly what Authority Content is and how it differs from the regular flavours of SEO, video and content marketing.

It's only by grasping the core concepts of Authority Content that you'll be able to create a bullet-proof marketing machine that won't crumble the first time a popular social media site loses traction or Google updates its algorithm.

So, what can you expect to find once you've turned the page? In a word: "everything". I'm giving you the entire strategy from start to finish, step by step, with nothing left out. I'm not the kind of guy who gives useful but incomplete information, like many other marketers do. I'm not going to be satisfied with just giving you the broad brush strokes. That just isn't the way I operate, and frankly, Authority Content won't work unless you have the entire picture. Although the strategy can be applied to any market, the precise implementation is always going to vary slightly – depending on your target market, product, service and objectives.

In fact, it's important to take this methodology, tweak it and make it your own. In this way you'll take ownership and make it work for you.

A common mistake I frequently observed in the stock market field that I used to work in was that people would be looking for the perfect trading system. Often referred to as the "Holy Grail," this system would tell them exactly when to buy and when to sell to make maximum profit every time. They were looking for a magic bullet to wealth. They'd go in search for this system and spend many thousands of dollars on books, courses and events and yet still fail to find what they were looking for. These people would then blame the strategy, then the teachers and eventually give up.

What they failed to realise is that there is no "push button" system for anything worthwhile. To make a success of any strategy, you need to learn the fundamentals, the underlying principles and how to adjust the approach to suit your situation.

What you'll find within the following pages are the fundamentals; the principles of how to market your products/services until your business becomes the market leader. This will take work – there are no short cuts – but trust me, the rewards are worth it. Turn this page only when you're prepared to learn Authority Content from start to finish.

Relax, this is a one-time exercise. Once Authority Content is burned into your brain, you'll have everything you need to implement it. Then adjust the sails as the winds change and enjoy an unstoppable flow of traffic, increased conversion rates and the coveted position of being recognised as an authority in your industry.

01. PREDICTING THE FUTURE

This is the part of the book that, if I'm not careful, could date faster than any other section.

It's important we talk about how the Internet as a medium has changed over the years and how the ways in which people interact with it are altering. But there's almost nothing I can say about how the Internet currently operates that doesn't risk becoming out-dated by the time you read this book.

I could try to offset this problem by throwing in a few predictions, but I'm not Nostradamus and I prefer to focus on fundamental truths. The rate of change in technology and online advancement has now increased to a point where it's actually quite risky to gamble on the short-term. And the Internet is littered with enough comments from astute individuals who got it very, very wrong.

- Thomas Watson, chairman of IBM, was quoted in 1943 as saying "I think there is a world market for maybe five computers." He couldn't have been more wrong and he was considered someone in the know.

- An author by the name of Clifford Stoll wrote an article in the mid-90s mocking the idea that people would ever want to buy stuff online. His arguments seem so blinkered and old-fashioned that it almost comes across as a comedy piece. Yet, at the time he wrote his essay, his findings sounded reasonable.[1]

- And, perhaps my favourite, in 1997, former Microsoft CEO, Nathan Myhrvold, said words to the effect that Apple, as a profitable business, was as good as dead. Maybe that one was just wishful thinking but, again, these were words from someone with knowledge and expertise in his market, but he was as incapable as just about everyone else in consistently and accurately predicting the future.

Predicting the future is a gamble and I don't gamble.

Little wonder then, that trying to figure out what sites and activities will be popular online next year is like trying to guess who's going to top the music charts in ten years' time. You could make a guess, and you might by fluke pick the right answer, but it's more likely that it'll be some new band that doesn't even exist yet.

The only thing I can say about the Internet that won't be out of date in a few weeks or months, and as clichéd as it seems, is …

"The Internet will evolve and it's going to keep on evolving."

I'm confident that whether you're reading this chapter in a few months, a few years, or even perhaps a few decades after it was written, that statement will continue to be true.

---

[1] http://www.newsweek.com/clifford-stoll-why-web-wont-be-nirvana-185306

Except for cats. The Internet will always be about cats[2].

Are You SURE You're Evolving?

The key point is that the unpredictability of Internet development is the only predictable thing about it. Which is why the "evolve or die" maxim continues to dominate in business and marketing circles. The need for a business to move and adjust with the times just to survive has always been true, but never on the scale that we've seen since the dawn of the Internet age.

Based on Moore's law, defined in the 1960s, Intel executive David House forecast that computer processing speed and power would double every 18 months. This forecast has held more or less true for almost 40 years in that industry and helps to explain the exponential growth in technology and why businesses must evolve simply to maintain the status quo.

But here's the real problem: too many businesses THINK they're evolving.

Moving with the times means adjusting your approach to suit the changing needs and attitudes of the market. Yet what most businesses do is create something that capitalises on current opportunities working in the here and now, and then totally demolish that approach when a new opportunity presents itself– starting all over again from scratch.

That's an opportunity seeker mentality and it's crazy. It would be like a business pumping time and money into developing a call centre, developing scripts and processes and then abandoning it

---

[2] Cats are the ultimate Internet meme.

after a year in favour of email marketing. Then, after investing heavily in this new approach, giving up on the concept and giving Google Adwords a go, only to give this up after a year, replacing that with search engine optimisation (SEO).

This type of thinking isn't evolution, it's slash and burn. It's a colossal waste of time and money and it places a huge strain on businesses, their owners and everyone who works for them.

But hang on. I've just laboured the point that the Internet changes rapidly. If not "slash and burn", what other choice is there to move with the times?

The other choice is to be a little more strategic in your thinking. Ask yourself, what does each new generation of Internet marketing have in common? Then, having identified the connection, develop a core strategy that will continue to work, despite unforeseen changes, with only a few minor adjustments to your tactics.

That's how business evolution is supposed to work. It's almost as if the speed at which the Internet develops has made everyone dizzy and caused them to lose focus on their overall objectives.

Google Still Exists, Right?

So, where do we start? How do we get that big picture view that allows us to make long-term plans that we don't have to completely abandon and redevelop every few months?

Let's start with Google.

Yes, I'm assuming Google still exists as you read this. There's always the possibility that Google will cease to exist at some point in the future, but it will inevitably be replaced by another company that gains the lion's share of users' attention.

Whether it's Facebook, YouTube or another platform, the thought process is the same. These companies gain the commitment of a large user base by offering free use of their platform in order to improve their users' online experience. Their primary focus is to serve the user and give them an experience they'll keep coming back for.

As their audience grows, they now have the eyeballs, and these platforms seek to monetise the attention by selling advertising space (in many different forms) to marketers and business owners like you and me.

So, although I'm going to be talking about Google a lot in this book, feel free to replace that name with whatever platform is current in your time and most relevant to your market.

But, anyway, as I was saying... it all starts with Google and, for the past decade or so, this has always been true.

Why? Because Google has the attention of a very large audience. The volume of people who pass through their sites (and I'm including their search engine, YouTube, Google Maps, Gmail and any other of the dozens of sites they operate) is mind-boggling and it's only natural that commercial entities want exposure to those eyeballs.

As you can imagine, appearing at the top of Google's organic search listing alone, for particularly valuable search terms, can be worth millions, if not hundreds of millions of dollars of revenue (literally). It makes sense when you consider how many eyeballs are watching Google. So it's no surprise that so many businesses, from the one-person outfit operating out of a garage to the international businesses with offices on every continent, have at least some interest in being noticed by Google to help serve up more customers.

Of course, this is easier said than done. Google has a limited amount of space on its search results pages and competition is fierce. As with most new media, in the early days, it used to be possible to find untapped, profitable niches and dominate them simply by virtue of being the only player in the space. However, windows of opportunities like that remain open for only a short space of time and now few, if any, of those niches remain.

To that challenge you can add Google's continuous refinement of its algorithm[3]. Its ability to change and adjust how it chooses which sites to rank is speeding up, and many who rely on traditional SEO for their traffic have to change tactics at an ever faster rate just to keep up. In many cases those chasing the algorithm have seen the bulk of their Google rankings wiped out in the space of weeks or even days with a single update.

Some bounce back, but it's getting harder and harder to manipulate the system. This is a classic example of how a business has to slash and burn its old tactics to find entirely new ones - rather than evolving and building on a solid foundation.

That doesn't mean SEO is a fool's errand; it simply means that

---

[3] A search engine's algorithm is the formula it uses to assess each web page and determine the keywords it should rank for, as well as the position in which it should rank each page.

many people's approach to SEO is the same as their approach to marketing in general: Short-term and opportunistic, rather than long-term and strategic.

There are only so many times any business can afford the time and cost needed to rebuild.

It's All About The Customers

Despite some people's assertion that SEO is doomed and Google wants to stamp it out, SEO is still an effective and profitable approach to traffic and lead generation. It's just that SEO isn't just about SEO anymore – SEO as a discipline has expanded to encompass so much more than just the traditional keywords and links. In many ways Authority Content can be described as a form of modern SEO. But it's such a different approach to the discipline that it requires a complete change in our thinking.

We must begin by reminding ourselves why we're tackling SEO in the first place. We don't aim to rank well for a specific keyword as if it's a badge of honour we can wear to parties. We aim to rank well so we can generate more traffic and get our products and services in front of more prospects and hopefully convert them to customers.

Customers: Remember them? They're the people we're aiming to serve. They're the people whose lives we believe we can improve with our product or service. SEO is not the endgame; SEO is just the method we use to help our business get maximum exposure.

Don't fall into the trap that many business owners do and become obsessed with the number of rankings and backlinks. Go back to the fundamentals and remember, "Why are you in business and whom are you looking to serve?" When we come to the practical elements of Authority Content, remembering who you're looking to serve is going to vastly improve your long-term success and have you focusing on what matters most.

You absolutely can serve the market better and improve Google's opinion of your website at the same time – but it always starts by focusing first on your clients. In fact, in my view, this is the ONLY truly effective, long-term approach.

The REAL Reason Google Exists

Believe it or not, Google's goals are the same as yours. Yes, the same as yours! They are not, as you might suspect, trying to ruin your SEO plans. Google's primary objective is to deliver the best and most relevant search results and in so doing, improve the service for their users.

Okay yes, now that they're a listed company, providing a return for their investors is probably their true primary goal. But achieving their financial targets is also tied up with being the best at delivering relevance. When someone visits a Google site and performs any kind of search, Google aims to understand what the person is looking for and then deliver the best answer it can find in the least number of clicks. Google's initial rise to fame was built on the back of this idea and in many ways, these fundamentals have remained the same. Google just keeps refining and improving their search technology.

None of this information about Google is likely to be a revelation to you, but if you've ever struggled with SEO or lost significant rankings after a Google update, it's probably because you forgot what Google is trying to do. When Google updates its algorithm, it's not doing it to make life hard for you, it's doing it to improve the experience of its visitors.

Never forget, Google doesn't exist to serve businesses. Google exists to serve its users.

It's a subtle difference but an important one nonetheless.

Let's consider a really obvious example. Once upon a time, Google's algorithm heavily weighted the importance of backlinks. It was possible to generate lots and lots of incoming links to your site containing specific keywords and Google would then rank your website well for those keywords. If your website was about repairing boats and you created loads of incoming links that used the text "repairing boats", your Google rankings improved for those search terms.

Then people identified the loophole and started to abuse this system. They spent huge amounts of time (and money) generating as many links as possible containing the keywords they wanted to rank for. It became possible for even poor quality sites, with little or no relevant content, to rank quite well using almost nothing but this strategy. If this had been left unchecked, eventually the quality of Google's search results would have been compromised and its ability to deliver relevant results would have been harmed.

So, Google updated its algorithm and if a site received an unusually high proportion of links containing the same keyword, this was deemed "unnatural". As a result, the benefit of many such links was discounted and in some cases, Google even penalised sites. Suddenly, generating scores of incoming links containing specific keywords was no longer enough to gain solid search engine rankings. The businesses that relied on this system for generating traffic had to scramble to update their backlink profile and create more links, with a greater variety of keywords.

But here's the interesting thing...

The websites that had lots of incoming links that were generated naturally by, for example, people linking to the website because they liked it, didn't lose ground. In fact, in most cases they moved up the rankings. The incoming links had a natural variety to the keywords in the links and so were largely unaffected by Google's update.

Think about what that means for a moment.

Websites where the owners spent massive amounts of time creating artificial links moved down in the search engine results. Websites that were popular because they had great content, moved up in the search engine results. Can you see how that fits into Google's prime directive? Google wants its search engine results to be full of sites that are popular for having great content – not businesses that have figured out how to game the system.

So the businesses that lost their rankings had two choices. They could either look for a new loophole to exploit and hope that Google wouldn't notice, or they could take a step back and figure out what Google is trying to accomplish... and then align their goals with Google's.

Basing a business model on a Google loophole is like building a house on the beach. It's only a matter of time before the tide comes in and washes it away. Focus on offering your customers and prospects a high quality experience and then suddenly life becomes a lot easier. Best of all, as Google's algorithm is refined, obtaining and retaining strong search engine rankings becomes easier, rather than progressively harder.

I don't know about you, but taking on Google and its army of world-class genius minds sounds like a suicide mission to me. If you can't beat them, join them.

Chapter 1 Exercise

- Take a few moments to review your company's mission statement (you do have one, right?) and consider how much of your marketing is truly aligned with your primary objectives.

  If you don't yet have a mission statement, complete the following sentence:

  We help *<insert target market and their problem>* by *<insert your solution>* so that they can *<insert your biggest benefit>*.

  For example, systemHUB.com's would be:
  We help *small and medium sized business owners remove themselves from the day-to-day operations of their business* by *systematising their core processes and storing them in the cloud* so that they can *build a profitable business that works without them*.

- Spend 20 minutes surfing on Google, and note how hard they're working to find smarter and faster ways to improve your experience and deliver great search results. Think about how you've seen Google evolve.

---

02. FINDING UNLIKELY SUCCESS (& REPLICATING IT)

It's 24th May 2003, and I'm in Melbourne. I'm shaking like a leaf while the room next door slowly fills up with people who have come to hear me present on the topic of using *Metastock*, a stock market charting software package. It was my first time speaking in public and I now know why people fear it more than death.

This wasn't exactly where I expected to be, just a few years after leaving school, but it turned out to be the beginning of my entrepreneurial journey, and the genesis of Authority Content.

I had decided against going to university when I left school and instead took out a $5k loan to complete a weekend-long stock-trading course that promised to make me a millionaire. I figured it was pointless to go to university for years to learn how to make money when I could just go straight to where I knew the money already was: the stock market.

Of course, I quickly learned that, in order to make money in the stock market, you needed to have some money to begin with. A $5k debt, living with my mum in a two-bedroom flat and stacking shelves in a supermarket wasn't going to cut it.

At the time I was heavily using *Metastock* software. A friend and I noticed that quite a few people in our little trading group were having trouble getting a grip on its complexities. We came up with the idea of creating a book called the *Metastock Programming Study Guide* that would help people make sense of the program.

At the start of the Metastock venture, I thought the same thing as I did when writing this book: "Why not?" I was a little more tech-savvy than most and I intuitively understood the software. We could help people and make some money at the same time. I took all the *Metastock* courses I could and then spent six months turning what I'd learned into a study guide.

The feedback from our immediate community was outstanding. People seemed to find what we'd produced really helpful. The only snag was that, as I have already pointed out, our community was small. If we were going to make any real profit from our months of hard work, we were going to have to learn how to market it to a wider audience.

Which is how I ended up in a room, sick with nerves, wondering if I could really deliver something that would be of value to all these people who had paid to hear me speak. The idea was to use the event to share some knowledge and at the same time, introduce people to our study guide.

Things went... *Okay* actually.

My delivery was pretty awkward, especially since I basically read my notes word for word for about an hour, making little eye contact with the audience. That made me look a bit like a kid trying to be a grown-up. But it was a huge, defining moment for me. I stepped out of my comfort zone and although I didn't realise it at the time, discovered the first few pieces of Authority Content. If you really, really feel the need, you can watch an excerpt of one of my first workshops here: www.authoritycontent.com/early-dave-video

Doing More Of What's Working

We continued to tour around Australia, conducting workshops. As I became more practiced and confident, the feedback from our attendees improved. But we still ran into the same obstacle, significantly expanding our audience and growing our customer base remained elusive, we needed to extend our reach somehow.

We had the idea of videoing our last workshop and maybe giving it away as a bonus to those who bought the study guide. It wasn't a fully formed idea but we figured we'd just record it and decide what to do with it afterwards. With hindsight, if all we'd done was to give away or sell the video, little would have come of it. But I somehow came up with the idea of chopping the video up into segments and posting them on YouTube (this was pretty cutting edge back in 2003).

That's when the magic started to happen.

The videos started getting views. A few thousand here, a few thousand there. Given that people looking for guidance on using *Metastock* was a fairly small niche of the larger group learning about how to trade the stock market niche, these numbers were amazing. Within a short space of time, one of the videos ended up with 45,000 views, we were on to something!

Not only was the *Metastock Programming Study Guide* a success, the first elements of Authority Content were falling into place.

The *Triple Your Trading Profits* course came next. I partnered with my co-author of the study guide, Stuart Mcphee and followed the same pattern. We created a product, we ran a workshop, we recorded it and we uploaded snippets to YouTube. In fact, we did this a whole bunch of times and that particular channel is coming up to having a few million views!

Admittedly there was a certain amount of good timing involved. Sometimes success in business is about being in the right place at the right time. Video was still something of a novelty and it was a little easier back then to capture a portion of the YouTube audience.

But don't start thinking that Authority Content is just a fancy name for YouTube marketing. Ploughing all your online marketing efforts into YouTube is just as dangerous as trying to exploit Google loopholes. YouTube was – and still is – a core part of this strategy, but if YouTube died a death tomorrow and was replaced by something entirely new and unforeseen, I could switch platforms with minimal effort and lose virtually no momentum in the process.

The Qualities of a Successful Business

The take-away from this story is that you don't need to spend huge amounts of money to market your business, you don't need to spend years in education and you don't need to obsess over getting every detail right the first time around.

A little bit of guile, a willingness to step out of your comfort zone, and a focus on delivering something of genuine value to your customers can take you a long way. Yes, this book is going to show you, step-by-step, how Authority Content can work for just about any business. I truly believe it can work for anyone with the following qualities:

1) A product or service that is genuinely great

You can't fake this. In the internet age, if you don't have a great product that you believe in 100%, no amount of marketing is going to earn you long-term success. Eventually the flaws in what you deliver will become common knowledge and your business will lose traction.

Profitability may be the end goal and it may be necessary to get your product into more people's hands, but you'll never achieve your objective if you're not also 100% committed to satisfying your customers and giving them something that is worth far more to them than whatever you're asking them to pay for.

2) The capacity for growth

If your business suddenly experienced a ten-fold increase in customers, could you handle the increased workload? This may sound like a nice problem to have but, if you're not prepared for it, your business can break in two. I've seen this happen when a business is featured on a "daily deal" website and suddenly they receive more customers than they were prepared to handle. The result is a huge volume of poor customer experiences that can be the death of a business.

3) A mind-set that is prepared for the long haul

It takes years to experience "overnight success", so you must be willing to think about the long term game and even be willing to make short term sacrifices for long term gain. If you're obsessed with short-cuts and loopholes, Authority Content isn't for you.

Evolve or die, remember?

If you get stuck using one strategy then it's only a matter of time before you come unstuck. It's easy to confuse skill and talent with being in the right place at the right time. If I reacted to my first successes by assuming I had discovered the perfect marketing formula for printing money, I would've gone bankrupt a long time ago.

I didn't do that. I used what I learned from my first success to develop a strategy that is capable of evolving and allows me to move from trend to trend. I don't have to compromise my fundamental vision of delivering valuable content that helps my target market achieve their own success.

Evolution, adaptation, rolling with the punches, whatever you want to call it, it must be a part of your business DNA. If it isn't, then this is the exercise you must complete before you turn the page.

Chapter 2 Exercise

- Review your product and service and identify whatever changes are necessary to improve the value it provides to your customers.

- Review your business and outline some steps that could give you extra capacity and allow you to cope with a substantial increase in new business.

- Ask yourself, honestly, if you're prepared to make changes and take on challenges that you might ordinarily go to great lengths to avoid. Don't turn the page until you've mentally steeled yourself to venture into the unknown.

03. STRATEGIC AUTHORITY

Three Big Obstacles

These days, the three biggest obstacles that you must overcome if you're going to make a success of your marketing are:

Attention, Engagement & Trust

I used to say getting attention and engagement was easy, yet trust was the biggest hurdle. But not anymore. Now, all three obstacles are critical and are getting harder to achieve.

Gone are the days of winning attention with "win any keyword with enough links" SEO and "10 cent clicks" with Adwords. Getting attention is becoming increasingly challenging as the background noise becomes louder and more pervasive.

Consider this, have you noticed how long it takes your good friends to reply to a text? It's taking longer these days! Even close friends whom you have known for ages might take hours to reply or even keep you waiting until the next day. People are busier than ever before. Whereas a text message was once an immediate attention-grabber, now it's competing with social media notifications and email updates, amongst countless other attention grabbers.

So, if it's hard to get the attention of those who know and love you, imagine how much harder it is to get the attention of those just out of arm's reach.

Similarly, engagement runs into a related problem. Even if you do manage to get someone's attention, how are you going to keep it? Whatever communication you send, people are going to judge it within a few seconds and, if it doesn't deliver value, they'll move on to something else.

And even if you get someone's attention and successfully engage them, they won't automatically trust you. Trust is something that takes time to build.

What's more, this concept of "trust" is a huge deal for Google at the moment. Their goal of providing people with the best and most relevant content is tied up in whether it can show its customers a link and be confident that the content on the other side is worthwhile. What's interesting about this challenge is that it is being addressed by considering the source of the content and whether or not Google believes the publisher is trustworthy.[1]

Attention, engagement and trust; these are the biggest obstacles you face in building your business. So this begs the question, what's the quickest way to power you over all three obstacles in one almighty leap?

---

[1] Source: Google's Quality Rater Guidelines cites the focus on sites that demonstrate expertise, authoritativeness and trustworthiness (EAT).

Authority Trumps Everything

When you're a recognised authority, your ability to grab people's attention, engage with them, and develop trust is instant and immeasurable. Think about industry leaders and experts – the kinds of people that draw a crowd whenever they have something to say. It's as if people are drawn to them. More often than not, from a business perspective, authorities get the lion's share of business and profits.

The definition of an authority is *someone or something with the power to influence others.* Some people naturally command authority by their demeanour or social status, while the rest of us have to earn that ability to influence by virtue of the knowledge we possess and our ability (and willingness!) to share it in a meaningful way.

If your product is relevant and useful, and if you're knowledgeable about your market, the only barrier to you becoming a recognised authority in your space is the way in which you communicate what you have to offer. Once you learn how to do this, everything will start to fall into place.

Authorities have no trouble getting **attention** because we know it's worth our while to listen when they speak. In fact, much of the time we deliberately seek out an authority and pay close attention.

Authorities have no problem **engaging** people because their status commands that people take the time to really listen to what's being shared.

Authorities find it easy to gain people's **trust**, almost by definition, because this role automatically implies that they are somebody trustworthy. If they weren't, it's unlikely that they would have risen to this position in the first place.

Once you're an established authority, people stop questioning whether you're worth their time, attention and trust. It's almost as if they skip over those steps and go straight to the more important question: is your product or service right for me?

As an authority, that question becomes far easier to answer.

I have worked hard at establishing my business and myself as an authority. As a result I have no difficulty generating leads. Then, when we chat on the phone, we decide together whether or not we're a good fit. That's the beauty of Authority Content. Often, whether the customer is chatting with a sales person, or placing an order online, it isn't about convincing the customer – they've already decided – it's about ensuring whether this transaction is going to be right for both of us.

There's no hard sell, no pushy salespeople cold-calling on my behalf, and there's definitely no agonising over which marketing tactic we'll try to exploit.

Wouldn't you love to be able to do away with all of that rubbish? You know what I'm talking about. They are those elements of marketing that everyone says are necessary but leave you feeling like you're trying to trick your way into a sale, or that you're just in a shouting match with the competition.

That's what strategic authority has done for me. It's enabled me to do away with all that rubbish and that's what it can do for you.

Yes, you can be strategic in your efforts to become an authority. No one becomes an authority in anything without some element of *creation*. The only question is whether a person in that position arrived there deliberately, or as an unintended consequence of their actions.

For example, the CEO of a Fortune 500 company may not have consciously set out to obtain authority, however often it can be earned as a natural consequence of being a savvy businessperson.

My point is this: manoeuvring yourself into a position of authority is wise and a highly effective way to market your business. I call it "strategic authority" since it's done with conscious thought and with planning.

If the idea of being an "authority" makes you anxious – don't worry. We're talking about a very specific kind of authority here and it doesn't necessarily put you in the spotlight (if being the centre of attention doesn't appeal to you). The type of authority I refer to is simply about positioning you or your business as the market leader, the most knowledgeable and valuable entity in your industry.

It's about answering the fundamental questions people ask when they visit a website…

Can this company help me solve my problems?

Can they deliver on their promises?

Do I trust this business enough to make a purchase?

Many marketers obsess over perfectly worded sales copy and Hollywood level production videos that demonstrate positive answers to these questions. There are more effective and efficient ways to be seen as an authority. That isn't to say that good sales copy and smart videos aren't important – they are – but once your authority level reaches a point, it's not dependent on marketing flourishes to win new customers.

So what makes an expert be seen as an expert?

Sure, some people build authority by chance - simply being in the right place at the right time. But who wants to rely on chance? You can be more strategic than that – let me show you how to become an authority with predictability. Becoming an authority won't be a matter of IF but rather a matter of WHEN.

Chapter 3 Exercise

- Grab a pen and paper and jot down all the experts, market leaders and authorities you can think of in your industry. It doesn't matter if they're individuals, businesses or some other kind of organisation.

- Next, for each name that you've written down, make a list outlining all the qualities they have which made you identify them as an authority. What have they done, said or published that has brought them to this status?

- I love this third exercise because it helps you get a sense of what's needed if you're going to build your own authority.

---

04. AUTHORITY CONTENT EXPLAINED

Authority isn't some mystical force that people either have or don't have. It's based on real, tangible elements that you can build or acquire to establish yourself in that position. Authority Content is simply the act of generating these elements and promoting them in a smart, systematic and scalable fashion.

I'm hoping that by now, you've already intuited what Authority Content is and speculated about how it works, but let me give you the full definition…

"Authority Content is the act of consistently creating and distributing helpful information and stories to gain attention, engagement and trust, for a clearly defined audience, with the objective of identifying who will benefit from your products and services."

That's a bit of a mouthful, so let's unpack that definition.

First of all, notice that Authority Content requires *consistent* action. Doing one round of videos or blog posts, for instance, isn't enough. Your content needs to be shared, steadily and consistently. That doesn't mean spending thousands of hours generating content. It's not about quantity, it's about consistency. If you only produce 12 pieces of content this year (and I'm going to show you how to easily repurpose it into way more than that), you'd be far better off releasing this content at the rate of one a month, rather than publishing it all in one go.

Notice also that the information you're creating and distributing is *helpful*. This is a big change for some old-school SEO practitioners. So, if that's you, start getting yourself into a mental attitude where you can let go of some old habits. Producing content is no longer just about satisfying Google; your content must be high quality with answers to the very specific questions that your clients and prospects are asking.

Great content marketed effectively will give you people's *attention*. A consistent flow of information that is genuinely useful and relevant will help you establish *engagement*. Authority Content takes it one step further and also seeks to gain the *trust* of that audience by attracting only those who are really going to benefit from your product or service.

The fact is, your products and services aren't for everyone. Sure you might be able to help a large group, but no solution is a perfect fit for everyone. This is really key, because as determined as you are to sell your product or service to the people who will benefit from it, you must be equally determined not to sell to those who aren't a good fit.

The Internet is just too transparent to get away with taking people's money and leaving them to discover that they probably would have been better taking a different route. If you sell someone on your product or service but don't meet their needs, word travels quickly. As a result, your ability to gain the market's trust and elevate yourself as an industry authority will be severely limited.

Turning Away Customers

A little while ago I had a phone call from a business coach who wanted me to "sell him" on the idea of SEO and why he should work with my company. Instead, after gaining a proper understanding of what his business needed, I "unsold him" and recommended he take his marketing down a completely different path.

Did he find that a little weird? Absolutely, but after talking things through, it became clear traditional SEO wasn't the best solution for him at that time. Just like a doctor, I first sought to understand his symptoms and then I prescribed the medicine that would help him the most... even though that didn't include our products or services! I also demonstrated to him that he could trust me and that I'm not in it for the quick buck. I only want to work with those whom I know I can help.

Now, every time this chap shares this "weird" story with his friends, colleagues and clients, my position as an authority is reinforced and he feels comfortable referring people to me, knowing I'm only going to do what's best for his clients. Obviously this changes the whole dynamic. It is just one small step towards becoming an authority.

Side note: Curious to hear an interview with this business owner? Visit: http://www.melbourneseoservices.com/business-accelerator/

So, what causes one person to be seen as the industry leader rather than 'just another company' in an overcrowded marketplace? What elements build up someone's authority?

Clearly there are a variety of factors but let's take a look at the three major elements you can use like a checklist to shortcut your road to authority.

Factor #1 – Core Authority

Core Authority is the most crucial of the three and requires some ongoing work. In short, it's about understanding your target market's problems and having the ability to articulate them better than they can. In this way, the assumption is also made that you must know the solution.

If you genuinely have knowledge, skills and expertise in your market, this should be a relatively easy task. Ask anyone who has worked in, and has a passion for a particular industry, what problems are faced by their clients, and you'll find they'll be able to tell you without having to refer to any notes. They just know and they can articulate this in great detail.

If you feel that your knowledge of your market is not quite up to that level, you either need to get your head down and study until you do, or you need to bring someone into your business who already has that level of expertise.

This is important because Authority Content isn't a "fake it till you make it" exercise. You can't establish authority for a person or a business that has nothing authoritative to offer people.

Step one of Core Authority is having a depth of understanding and to truly know your market and the issues it faces. Step two is about having a body of work to deliver that message. Having a good amount of content, whether it's emails, blog posts, videos, podcasts or any or all of the above, shows you're more than a "fly by night, make a quick buck" operator. It shows you're in it for the long term.

With a large body of work your knowledge seeps into every type of communication that you engage in and on a subconscious level (or even on a conscious level), your audience will have a strong sense that you "get" them. They will see that you understand their experiences and their challenges – and the further they research you or your business the more this is reinforced.

Authorities have opinions, authorities educate, and authorities care about their community. You need a body of work that demonstrates these qualities. It will grab attention, engage people and earn people's trust.

Factor #2 – Website Authority

Adjusting your website to reflect your authority may sound obvious but it's too crucial a factor for it to go without saying. The fact is, these days, before someone does business with you, one of the first things they're going to do is Google you and your business and study your website to see if there is a congruent message to match what they know about you already.

Which means – surprise, surprise – your website needs to have the content we talked about in core authority (e.g. blog posts, videos, podcasts) and it needs to be professionally displayed.

A skinny website with an "About Us" page and a list of your products or services isn't going to get the job done. It starts with telling great stories. People in all cultures, engage with stories and it always surprises me that people don't use this approach more. An "About Us" page that tells the owner's personal journey and experiences through the market is always going to be more effective than a dry discourse on the year the firm was established, the awards it has won and so on.

If you've ever watched any of my videos or read any of my articles you'll already know that I use story telling in all my communication. It's one of the ways I'm able to differentiate myself from my competitors. My visitors can quickly learn about who I am, how I got to where I am and see the proof I have the business chops to help them.

Sharing relatively personal information about my career and my life presents me as an open and honest person and really helps to boost the "trust" element of my authority. This isn't a fake or calculated effort to convince people that I'm trustworthy – people see through that – but by just being willing and able to tell my story, I can share something that people can relate to.

Telling stories is easy. We all know how to do it, instinctively. Copywriting is hard to do and takes time to learn, but we all know how to tell our stories and it's just a matter of getting it down in writing or on video. Once again, if you know your market and you have experiences to share, simply relating them to your target audience will create a real affinity.

However, Website Authority isn't just about telling stories and demonstrating your Core Authority – it also includes how you present your information. You don't need to break new ground and create a website that is some kind of technological miracle but it must be smart, professional-looking and above all, consistent.

Apple is a great example of this consistency in its marketing. Whether you're watching an Apple video, browsing the Apple website, or reading an email from Apple, everything about Apple is congruent. Style, voice and even font, are all consistent and are quickly identifiable as coming from the same source. There's no point in building an extensive body of helpful content if people can't connect the dots and recognise that it's coming from the same brand, whether that's you or your business.

You can't position yourself as an authority if your content isn't marketed in a way that ties it altogether. So, don't neglect the layout and styling of your website. Invest in it, test it and polish it to a high sheen.

Factor #3 – Social Authority

Social Authority is the third component and presents proof of your authority. It's someone else – whether a customer or another recognised authority – standing up and saying that you're an expert and you're someone who is deserving of people's attention, engagement and trust.

One of my favourite ways to demonstrate Social Authority is with case studies that tell stories about a specific customer. A visitor comes along and reads a story about one of your customers who was going through exactly the same problems that they're currently facing. They learn about the steps you took to help them overcome their obstacles and it's only natural then to visualise what it would be like for them to experience the same assistance.

This social proof is powerful, really powerful. A case study, related clearly and honestly, demonstrates to your visitors that you have what they're looking for.

So where do these case studies and testimonials come from? Occasionally someone will offer you one but if you want to create an overwhelming collection from a wide variety of people, you're going to have to ask for them.

Depending on your cultural background and your personality type, this might be difficult for you to do, but you're going to have to suck it up and get used to doing it. The truth is that, if you're worthy of being an authority in your space because your products and services are of a high quality and deliver on the promises made by your marketing, most people are delighted to provide you with a written or video testimonial.

I believe gathering case studies needs to be woven directly into your work processes, so you don't even have to think about it. Every time you satisfy a customer, the next step in your workflow should be to ask them if they'll jump on Skype with you and record a testimonial. It's one of the best ways to quickly build trust and be viewed as an authority.

It makes sense when you think about it. You don't have to tell people you're an authority when you've got dozens of people who are willing to say it for you.

I've collected over 200 testimonials for my businesses and it's reached the point where it just made sense to collate them altogether onto one website (www.daveraves.com).

I don't expect people to read or watch every testimonial but being able to point people to a site where they can find this huge volume of Social Authority, is incredibly powerful.

Yes, it takes a while to get to this number of testimonials but like everyone else who collects testimonials, I started out with just one. So start collecting testimonials today.

As you can see, Social Authority is about showcasing the fact that other people already know, like and trust you.

Another way to do this is to link to your active social media profiles – the ones where you've taken the time to build a reasonable number of followers and engagement. Linking to your Facebook page that has 1,000 likes doesn't, on its own, establish you as an authority, but it's another piece of the puzzle. It shows that others already care enough to listen to what you have to say and it shows you're a helpful, useful, relevant and an authoritative business.

Your "Authority Scoreboard"

I've grouped authority areas into three broad categories. In practice, your customers judge your level of authority on a myriad of different factors but they all primarily come under these three headings. On a subconscious level, your customers score you based on each of these factors, totalling these up on their internal "Authority Scoreboard" and adopting a view of you and your business based on the sum of these elements.

If I were to list every possible factor that impacts your "Authority Score," not only would this book be twice as thick, it would also be deeply discouraging, representing a level of work that most of us do not have the resources to tackle.

But, here's the secret…

Each authority factor carries a *different* weight. One endorsement from an existing authority, for example, could be worth ten times more points on your scoreboard than having a professionally-designed logo on your website's homepage.

The key is to identify the factors that carry the highest number of authority points in relation to the amount of time and money required to integrate them into your business and marketing strategy. This is what Authority Content does so well because, as you'll see in the next section, it allows you to hit the maximum number of these authority factors all at once!

We've completed a pretty comprehensive overview of what Authority Content is, why it works and how it works. Starting in the very next section, we're going to begin working our way through the specific, practical steps you need to take to put this system into practice within your business.

Chapter 4 Exercise

You're going to give yourself a head start on some of the steps described in the remainder of this book by taking an inventory of your existing authority assets and keeping it handy while you read the remaining pages. You may already have a lot of existing content that can be repurposed without the need to start from scratch.

Depending on the size of your business, you may be able to make this list of assets on your own or you may need to enlist the help of one or more of your colleagues. Either way the exercise is simply to list everything physical and digital that you own that is, in one form or another, a type of marketing asset. Here are a few examples to get you thinking along the right lines:

- o Customer feedback emails
- o Unused video footage (interviews, seminars, testimonials, case studies, etc.)
- o Unpublished articles
- o Articles published in print media (such as local press)
- o Awards or accolades that you or your business have won
- o Photos of your business or of industry-related events you've attended.

Many businesses have collected a wealth of what I call "Authority Assets" and don't even realise what they are or why they're of value. Don't worry if you're struggling to understand why these assets are important; you will soon enough. For now, just make the list and keep it handy.

---

05. PRESENT, PRODUCT, PROMOTE

When I was a kid I was in the Scouts. The Scout Leaders used to come up with games to try to keep us occupied. In one of these games the Scout Leader would call out "four minutes!" and the aim of the game was to try to guess when four minutes were almost up and then we'd sit down. Whoever sat down the closest to four minutes, without going over, was the winner.

We'd play this game in the Scout hall where there were no clocks and no external ways of keeping track of the time, so the idea was to try to count the seconds in your head. Try it sometime; it's actually pretty hard to do. The brain is very good at expanding or contracting our sense of time passing.

Of course, the real aim of the game was to keep everyone quiet for four minutes while we concentrated on counting silently, but that's beside the point. The reason I'm telling you this story is because one of my friends, Adam, used to win this game almost every single time. He was so good at the 'four minutes' game' that some people stopped trying to count and just sat down when he did.

They didn't know why he was better at the game than everyone else; they just figured that if they copied him they'd be successful.

Some people spend their whole life doing that. They try to imitate successful people without trying to understand precisely why they're so good at what they do. That only gets you so far. All those kids copying Adam thought they were being smart, but what would they have done if Adam were at home sick, or if he decided he was bored with winning and just stopped playing and moved onto something else?

Fortunately, Adam was bad at keeping secrets. He eventually revealed that his technique was to rock back and forth, using his steps as a kind of pendulum for keeping his mental counting even and consistent. It wasn't long before everyone played 'four minutes' by rocking around the hall and the game was eventually killed stone dead. The Scout Leaders banned this technique, but that's a whole other story.

There are two great lessons I take from that memory. The first is that if I'm going to show you how to be successful at marketing your online business, I need you to understand exactly what Authority Content is and why it works, instead of just jumping straight into the actionable steps. Hopefully I've already got you to that place, but if you've skipped ahead in the book, please go back and read the first few chapters. I can give you the fundamentals, and I can give you the steps, but you need to understand both if you want to get ahead.

The second lesson – and I believe this can be applied in so many different areas of life – is that even when it appears as if you're operating on a level playing field and even when there appears to be substantial competition, there are always ways to swing the odds dramatically in your favour. You just need a good system to follow.

So here's my system for building authority in any niche.

What are the "3 Ps" of Authority Content?

We've already talked quite a bit about the importance of creating relevant content. Obviously this is a challenge. There are plenty of people out there who already know the importance of this strategy but fail to make any headway because content creation is time-consuming and expensive…

Unless you're following the Authority Content system, of course!

The system I'm about to outline enables you to create a simple, straightforward process for conceiving, planning and delivering high quality content all year round. Yes, it still requires some effort and a little investment, but it removes the challenges of trying to figure out what to create and ensures that you don't procrastinate or become paralysed by indecision.

The framework in which I'm going to introduce this system is called the "Three Ps" (3Ps), and as you might expect from the name, it consists of three simple steps:

- Present

- Product

- Promote

These three steps in themselves are not the real secret behind Authority Content (we'll get to this in a moment), but they allow us to consider the work we're going to do in a clear, logical fashion.

"Present" is about batching your content creation, capturing as much quality, in-depth, rich content as we can in the shortest possible time and for the least amount of money.

"Product" is how we package that content into something valuable that people can easily access. It answers questions such as, in what format do we deliver it, how much we charge our customers or do we give it away for free.

"Promote" is simply about optimising the content and getting it consistently in front of your clients and as many prospects as possible.

The third and final step, the promotion of your content, is probably what you were expecting the majority of this book to be about and, quite possibly, the skills you're most eager to learn. However, "Promote" doesn't work unless you've really nailed the first two steps. In fact, the better the job you do with the first two steps, the easier the marketing element becomes.

When you get all three steps working properly you'll create a traffic and conversion machine that is profitable for you AND beneficial for the customer. Never forget that our goal and motivation is to add value to people's lives. We're not going to simply create low quality articles and rewrite them numerous times for the sake of it, hoping to pick up a few links and trying to fool Google. We're going to create truly great content, package it up into lots of different formats and share it with the people who need it most.

Most SEOs get it wrong by pumping out content for the primary sake of building links, while most content marketers get it wrong by putting out great content with little regard for optimisation. Authority Content lives in the intersection between great SEO and content marketing.

That's how we Google-proof, search engine proof and future proof our work.

Please understand that this strategy takes work. Nothing worthwhile comes without at least a little effort but the rewards are worth it.

The Key To Success

In this section we're going to answer the question that's raised by the first of the 3Ps: "Present". How do we create the maximum amount of content with the minimum amount of time and money?

Let's say, for example, that you want to create a dozen videos. You rent a studio or set up your own – which doesn't come cheap. You want to maximise your output, so you spend several days writing and polishing your script. The video has to look right and you're not used to talking to a camera, so it takes you a dozen takes to get the first video right.

You've just spent a week and a chunk of cash to create one video, and you still have another 11 to produce!

At that rate, it's going to take you months to get your first batch of videos completed, and you haven't had time to even think about creating other forms of content, such as articles, ebooks, podcasts or infographics. Heck, you don't even have enough time in the day to return a text from a friend, let alone put aside a week to create some content.

But there is a better way, the Authority Content way... you're going to organise a workshop/live event. I say "workshop", but it doesn't really matter in what format you run the event. It can be a classroom-style workshop, a small interactive training session at your office or a VIP day for your best customers at a local hall. The key is to have a set date when you're getting together some people from your target audience and then delivering some useful and relevant content.

I had to explain a little there since I always run the risk of losing a certain percentage of my audience when I use the word "workshop". Immediately some people start thinking, "No, that isn't going to work for me."

If that's the thought running through your head, I need you to push that to one side for now and pay careful attention to the next few chapters. Why? Because it doesn't matter what excuse you might have for thinking that you're the exception and that this won't work for your business. That's all they are - excuses.

Excuses are bad for business. They're constructs that you use to give yourself permission to avoid doing something you might not want to do. Be honest with yourself. Your reasons for rejecting the idea of putting on a workshop – are they genuine challenges or are they just excuses?

How can you tell? If they're challenges, you'll find ways to overcome them. If they're excuses, you'll close your mind off to the possibilities of how it might work and insist that there's no way of tackling them. That's how you'll know.

I could have come up with plenty of excuses for believing that running a workshop to promote my *Metastock* guide was unworkable. I'd never conducted a workshop before. People wouldn't listen to me because I was too young. I didn't know exactly what I'd talk about and if people would be interested in attending. I didn't have a venue.

However, I was convinced that running a workshop was the way forward and so I found ways to overcome those obstacles.

For most people, excuses for not wanting to hold a workshop are simply a mask for not wanting to admit that speaking in front of a room full of people terrifies them. But that can be overcome with good preparation and practice. If you have a genuine, insurmountable phobia of public speaking, you can always get someone else in the business to do it, hire someone to handle the presentation on your behalf or just facilitate the event with other experts.

Whether you have reasons or excuses, please just put a pin in all of them for now. Let's instead focus for a few minutes on the reasons holding a workshop is actually a really good idea.

- The simple act of holding a workshop will elevate you and your business in people's eyes and will represent a giant step forward in establishing you as an authority.

- You can record the workshop and, in a single day, generate hours of useful video content.

- You can ask attendees to record a testimonial at the end of the session or during the lunch break, gifting you with potentially dozens of high quality endorsements, again in a single day.

- Your attendees will post to social media sites during the day, creating a buzz around your event and business.

- When you get a group of clients together in one room, the collective wisdom will produce amazing insights, helping you to generate ideas for expanding and improving your products and services.

- Many of the customers who attend your workshop will be transformed into dedicated, life-long, hard-core fans who will rave to others about you and your business.

- Invite your staff to attend the workshop and they'll develop a better understanding of your products and services.

- Setting a date for your workshop helps you to avoid procrastination and forces you to get on with the task of creating a written structure for whatever it is you're going to share.

Those are all great reasons for demonstrating that conducting a workshop is an excellent idea. However one of the most important benefits of holding a workshop is that, after the event, you'll have hours of video content that you can slice up into useful content blocks and post online, gradually over the next few months, or even over the period of a year.

One content-rich workshop can easily produce 30-40 videos and fuel your content marketing efforts. Because the videos are in a workshop setting, in a teacher-and-students format, this content naturally appears more authoritative than if it were just you in a studio, talking to a camera.

Running a workshop is a game changer for everyone I know who has ever invested the effort needed to put one together. It's enabled me to move into, and dominate, three highly competitive spaces: The *Metastock* industry, the SEO industry and the web video industry.

All three sectors are packed with individuals and businesses selling training and "done for you" services. SEO training and services, especially, are incredibly competitive. Yet I've been successful in all three fields by following almost exactly the same strategy.

Organise a workshop, record the event, and then use the video footage to create authoritative content that I can syndicate around the web to position me as an authority and create a consistent flow of new leads and clients.

Overcoming Your Objections

If you're willing to push aside any reservations you may be feeling and follow me as I take you through the 3Ps, you'll turn on a traffic and lead-generating machine that is unstoppable and, more crucially, is flexible enough to work in any industry and adapt to any changing circumstances.

That's all the good stuff about this part of Authority Content, but it's only fair that I circle back to some of the concerns that might have surfaced earlier. Let's take a look at some of the most common objections people have to conducting a workshop and provide another perspective.

Objection #1 - Workshops aren't suitable for my business

I get this one a lot. Maybe the product or service you provide just doesn't fit with the idea of 20 people in a room watching a PowerPoint presentation. It's a fair point, but you just need to think laterally.

First of all, although we think of a workshop as being in a classroom setting, that doesn't have to be the case. For our purposes, a workshop has a very broad definition and simply means getting a group of your target audience together in the same physical location on a specific date.

If you train horses, your classroom could be a stable. If you sell plant food, your classroom could be a vegetable garden. If you sell fishing excursions, take a group of students fishing.

As long as you can get everyone together in the same place, ready to learn something and you have room for someone with a video camera, you're conducting a workshop.

Objection #2 - I don't know what to teach

This is also a good objection but is also easily fixed with lateral thinking and a healthy dose of creativity. For my first workshop, promoting my *Metastock Programming Study Guide*, it was easy to come up with a curriculum. We simply expanded on the content we'd already created. However, I agree that not all businesses translate quite so easily.

The key is to get back into the mind of your customers and think about the problems they're facing and the amazing things you can teach them to help solve those problems.

When I began creating workshops for my SEO services, I knew that what my customers really wanted to know was how to drive more traffic to their website and business and ultimately they wanted to know how to market themselves better online. So that's what I taught them. It might seem strange to some that I would teach people how to do SEO for themselves when my business was about providing those services, but I think that's small-minded thinking.

The fact is, start-up business owners often can't afford a "done for you" service and would happily pay a smaller fee to attend a workshop and learn how to do this for themselves. Or pay a little less and receive a video recording of the workshop.

For more established businesses, our videos help to educate about the value our business offer provides. Most probably don't recognise the work required to do great SEO. So, once they review my videos and articles they often decide they'd rather hire us to do the work anyway.

This approach is used by many different service providers. A one-day workshop demonstrating how to do something can simultaneously be an opportunity to show that your services solve a time-consuming, complex problem, and are well worth investing in. You just have to get over your hesitation of letting people peek behind the curtain and see how you do what you do.

As I said before, I've always taken the counter intuitive approach of revealing everything, from A to Z and this mind-set has helped my business grow exponentially rather than hold it back.

So, we've covered training businesses and service-providing businesses. But what if you sell a range of products or even a single product? How do you turn that into a workshop?

The answer in this case is to push your product into the background and focus on the related needs of your customer base. If they're a customer, or a potential customer, ask yourself what related subjects would they be interested in learning about?

If, for example, you sell car wax, you could run a workshop on basic car maintenance. If you sell plant food, how about a workshop on creating and tending a vegetable garden? If you sell horse grooming kits, how about a day spent in a stable learning how to care for your horse?

So, whether you sell training, services or products, there are always topics of interest to your target market.

Don't worry if compiling content for your first workshop is a bit of a challenge. With each event you organise, you'll become more confident in your abilities, more attuned to your audience and more capable of identifying and serving the needs of your market.

Objection #3 – I'm a terrible public speaker

This objection doesn't apply if you've never tried it. If you're simply assuming that you're not up to scratch, I'd encourage you to at least give it a try before you decide it's not for you. Putting your face front and centre, not just on the day of the workshop but also in the video content that you'll subsequently be distributing online, may be essential if you're a key part of your company's branding. Remember, success is sitting just outside of your comfort zone.

Even if you feel like you have tried and failed as a public speaker, stick with it. No one was ever born a natural public speaker. It takes time and practise to improve – like all things in life. If you're building a business, growing a team and making a difference in the world, it's a skill worth mastering.

If you're still fighting the point, perhaps for your first workshop, you could consider promoting someone within your organisation to be the public face of your business. They don't necessarily have to have public speaking experience – although that would obviously be a plus – but if they're knowledgeable and passionate about your product, they're more than half way there.

Alternatively, you can hire a local celebrity or partner with a business that is in the same market but serves a different need. There are plenty of options for finding alternative speakers but again, I must emphasise, please only replace yourself as one of the speakers as a last resort.

Objection #4 – I'm new to the industry and no-one knows who I am. Why would they come to my workshop?

Naturally, putting on an event is always easier if you have an existing customer base, however that isn't a prerequisite for hosting an event. If you're a newcomer to the field, you can push your way to the front of the pack by partnering with one or more established businesses.

Identifying potential partners is a case of finding that sweet spot between (1) large enough to have an existing modest-sized audience and (2) small enough that they would welcome the promotional opportunities provided by attending your event. The key is to find a handful of existing authorities to get involved, so everyone has the opportunity to get in front of a wider audience than they already have access to.

Another option is to partner with a related charity and run the workshop as a fund-raising event in which all proceeds go to the charity. The charity provides you with legitimacy and an audience. You provide your expertise and a reason for people to attend.

Partnering with other experts and organisations also has value in that you'll be able to add to your authority status by virtue of being connected to the people who already have status in your field. In fact, even if you're an existing authority in your field, it may be well worth your while considering the partnership route for your event for this reason alone.

Chapter 5 Exercise

In the next couple of chapters we're going to go through the steps required to prepare and present your workshop so, for now, sit down with your business colleagues, or a trusted friend, and brainstorm ideas for:

- o   The content and theme of your workshop.
- o   Potential partners to participate.
- o   Possible venues and locations.

You don't need to make any firm decisions yet, but you want to have a few ideas ready before getting to the serious planning stage.

06. HOW TO PREPARE

If right now, planning a workshop feels like a colossal amount of work and too complex, expensive and time-consuming, then you're probably over thinking it.

You're not planning a convention or even a seminar… you're planning a workshop.

It can be as simple and as low-tech as you need it to be.

So forget all your thoughts about hiring expensive conference rooms and high-end audio visual teams. You're getting way too far ahead of yourself. I'm going to say this now and I'm going to keep repeating it at frequent intervals.

Keep It Simple.

Forget the preparation for a moment and instead, figure out your objectives. What, at a minimum, do you want to accomplish with your workshop? Your answer is probably going to look a bit like this:

Spend one day speaking to at least half a dozen people.

- Record the event.

- Break even on any costs.

- For now, that's about it.

In years to come, when you're really good at this, maybe you can think about hiring an expensive hall, filling it with a hundred eager delegates and making a tidy profit. But for your first workshop, keep it simple.

You might already have a room in your office that will serve nicely as a temporary classroom. Failing that, make a few calls to hotels or even local businesses that you know have suitable rooms and see if you can strike a deal. Once you've got a price you can afford, go ahead and book it for a date that is not more than a few months away. Now you're committed to following through.

Booking a venue becomes a positive constraint and forces you to get organised! There's nothing like the thought of a room full of clients and prospects to ensure you stay focused.

You now only have three things to arrange – inviting people to attend, preparing the content you're going to present and arranging someone to record the event.

Inviting People To Your Workshop

Begin with the invitations, even before you start preparing the content! You want to give people plenty of advance warning about the event so they have time to make arrangements to attend.

The good news is that you don't need a huge number of people to attend your first workshop, so you can afford to be choosy. Start out by inviting your best clients and any prospects you're keen to close. Make it a very exclusive, invitation-only event and make sure they feel special just by receiving the invitation.

Don't laugh, but if you're just starting out, you can also invite family, friends and work colleagues to fill the room.

The video camera is going to be pointed at you anyway and all viewers will see of your attendees is the back of their heads. They're not going to know (or care) who these people are, so make it easy on yourself and fill your room with anyone you can.

Hopefully you remembered to keep it simple and you've chosen a room that only seats a limited number of people, making it easy to get enough people together.

Inviting relevant authorities to come along and say a few words is also very effective. Whether they're going to deliver a 20-minute Q&A or a full-hour presentation, it gets an extra body in your room, adds to the authority of your workshop and makes it easier for you to fill the day with relevant content. Be strategic and think long term. Who would you love to build a business relationship with? Asking someone to speak at your event is a great door opener.

Next up, one thing you will definitely need, whether you're inviting a few hand-picked clients, emailing your entire database or inviting other experts, is a simple web page that describes and promotes your event. Even now, after running so many of these events, I like to keep this really simple. For my last workshop, I went down to the local pub and recorded a 5-minute video in which I described a problem, announced that I was running a workshop to solve it and explained what to do if the viewer wanted to attend.

You might be wondering, should you charge for attending? I would say so. Giving away tickets as part of a competition or as a bonus for making an expensive purchase is an option but I would still recommend charging something for your tickets. Your objective is to break even, so you don't need to charge the earth. But making it a paid event will also give the content a greater perceived value and make it easier to sell the material in different formats later on.

It also encourages people to attend. If the event is free, they are not losing anything if on the day, something else crops up last minute that demands their attention. People feel more compelled to attend if they've put some money down.

Finally, promoting your landing page can also be kept sweet and simple too. I hope you're getting the theme here. I like to build a little anticipation with a couple of teaser emails to your database or any partners you may have involved. Then send another promotional email announcing that the landing page is live, complete with an "early bird" offer in which the visitor can purchase a ticket for a heavily discounted price if they act quickly.

I'll set the "early bird" offer to expire after a week or two. Not only does a deadline encourage people to act, but it also trains them to respond when I make future time-sensitive offers. Once people realise that my deadlines are real and not gimmicks, they tend to respond quickly and take future offers seriously.

I'd also suggest a few personally emailed invitations to friends and colleagues can be a great way to get those initial tickets sold. Of course, there are a variety of ways to sell tickets to an event (Facebook, Adwords, remarketing, joint ventures) but for your first event, I'm confident you can get 5-20 people from your own existing network. Remember, just running the event is one part of the larger strategy, so you don't have to stress over numbers.

Preparing The Workshop Content

In tandem with your promotions, it's a good idea to solidify, or at the very least get more detail on, the topics you plan to cover.

Now there are any number of directions to head but it's always best to start with your target market in mind. What problems, questions and interests do they have that are associated with your products and services? You could even think about your industry as a whole and identify some of the issues surrounding it.

Another effective approach is to think about what your target market might be thinking and/or doing that would prompt them to seek out products and services similar to yours and what content would be most relevant to them at that point.

Whether you sell products or a service, will also influence the topics. For example:

Service Providers: Could present a workshop that teaches people how to do for themselves some, or all, of the services that you provide. That is, it could condense your entire method into one "crash course".

Product Vendors: Could present a workshop that teaches people something related to their area of interest, and that gives you, even if only in a small capacity, an opportunity to demonstrate your product.

Whichever direction you take, always remember the content you create will become the "bait" used for attracting prospects to your business. Selecting the right content upfront will determine who will, and will not, discover you online when we start the promotion stage – so it's important to spend a little extra time here.

Also, keep in mind you will save yourself a lot of time and effort further down the road if you make a point of creating a workshop agenda that, as much as possible, is evergreen - that is, something that won't date quickly. You'll struggle to repurpose your workshop content over the next year if it's out of date within a few months or even weeks.

If at this point you're still having trouble thinking of some topics, one of the best things you can do when faced with a marketing dilemma is to ask your existing clients and prospects what they'd like. A simple survey or quick phone call to your best clients asking, "If I were to put on a small training workshop, what topics would you find most interesting?" can uncover some great ideas.

Now, take all of these ideas and note them down, and once the initial brainstorming is done, you can organise it into a logical sequence. I like to think of this as if I'm writing the content of a book. I ask myself, what would make sense to come first? Perhaps an introduction outlining the day, who it's for, what are some of the problems you're going to solve, and what they can expect.

This can be followed by a combination of frequently asked questions, product demonstrations and case studies, explaining the process your business goes through to deliver a great product or service. I arrange such topics in the order that makes most sense. Sometimes, when I'm coaching clients through this process and depending on their business, I suggest they go wider and talk about other topics related to their industry. This is often the case for very product-driven businesses. It can also make sense to bring in other authorities and experts to cover some of these areas too.

With a rough outline, and a good idea of who might present what, it's time to get to work fleshing out sub-bullets of the most important points you'd like to cover under each topic. Choosing areas where you know your stuff and/or are passionate about it, makes this process that much easier. More often than not, you're just presenting what you know, and while you might not appreciate its value, your audience will.

For me, the last step is to turn these topics and bullet points into slides. Obviously you'll only need to do this for your own presentations and your other speakers will work on theirs. Work closely with your fellow presenters, especially if they're not employees. Keep them aligned to the objective of the day. It's about delivering value, recording some great content and expert positioning. It's not about how many products and services can be sold at the back of the room.

Find A Videographer

I would also recommend finding a videographer to record the event. I have had clients try to do this themselves, but unless you are a videographer, its more trouble than it's worth. I understand that sometimes when you're just starting out you're trying to keep your costs down. However, this is the one part of the process that must be done correctly. Why? Because the recordings will be the biggest asset from the event. If the audio quality is bad or the picture looks budget, you'll regret it.

For the sake of a few grand, hire a professional or, at the very least, go to a local university and find a final year student who's keen to build their portfolio. I would recommend, at a minimum, a two-camera setup, wireless lapel microphones for the presenters and one roving microphone.

It's important to capture all the action including any questions from the audience. There's nothing worse than watching a workshop recording where you can't hear an attendee's question and the presenter just goes on to answer it. It really just makes that part of the footage unusable.

Remember, the footage will become the core asset that we'll end up repurposing and syndicating around the web, so a good quality recording will make your life that little bit easier further down the line.

And with that, you're just about past the point of no return.

Chapter 6 Exercise

- Don't spend time thinking up reasons to talk yourself out of doing this. Book a room or a space and start sending out some invitations. Once you're committed to a specific date you'll be amazed at what you can achieve.

- Once your workshop venue and time is set in stone, build a landing page and start promoting it, plan ahead and put aside time each week to work on your content.

You should also aim to finish reading this book before your event begins. This will help you understand what you need to accomplish on the day of your workshop in order to make the following stages successful.

07. PRESENT YOUR AUTHORITY

Ok, you're all set now. You've booked a room, outlined the day, have half a dozen or more people attending and you're making things easy on yourself by keeping it simple.

Your attendees are paying to hear your solutions and although fancy workbooks, room decorations and gourmet snacks may sound appealing to you, they're not really important and just give you extra things to worry about.

Especially for your first workshop, your priority is to deliver your content and get it all on camera.

So try and relax. Easier said than done, I know, but there really is very little that can go so badly wrong that it ruins the day. Accept that some things are going to work better than others and that some things never quite go as planned and just be prepared to roll with it.

Every mistake you make on the day – and mistakes are always inevitable when you're trying something new – is a lesson learned that will make your next workshop that much more successful.

Now, one of the first things I like to do is create an itinerary for the day covering who's speaking on what, when and for how long. This helps give you a little structure.

I'd also suggest having either a staff member or family member helping out with the administration on the day too. They can check people in, ensure attendees sign video release forms, answer any questions, take photos, post on social media and ensure everything runs on time. This will mean you can remain focused on delivering great content.

I could fill a book with workshop anecdotes and tips, but there are really only three things that apply to every type of workshop that I would consider to be absolutely crucial.

1. Practise, practise, practise

If it's your first time and even if it's not, I'd strongly recommend getting in as much practise as you can before the event. The truth is, even the most natural and seemingly spontaneous performances from professional speakers, actors and even comedians are all well rehearsed.

You know your content, you're an expert in your field and I'm confident that, with a little extra preparation upfront, you're going to nail it!

2. Test All Your Equipment on the Day

If you have access to the workshop room in advance, run a few practise sessions, not just so you can hone your delivery, but also so you can test your video camera setup.

If you don't have access to the room until the day, arrive as early as possible to run some quick screen tests. Recording the workshop is such a crucial part of the Authority Content that this is the one thing you'll want to ensure goes smoothly.

Your professional videographer will no doubt have this covered but it's always good to double check. Do all the microphones, cameras and computers have full batteries? Do you have spare batteries? Have you got more than enough storage for all of the content?

If you're using a laptop to show your slides, will you need a projector and a clicker to change the slides? Running a few tests before and on the big day should ensure you've got everything covered.

I'd also recommend creating yourself a checklist so you remember everything or just visit www.authoritycontent.com, sign up for the home study course and you can have a copy of our checklist!

3. Get Testimonials and Photos

Now, as you'll learn by going through this book, I like to get the most out of every opportunity I can. I ask myself, "How can I get even more from running this event?" With that mind-set, you'll want to capture everything from testimonials to photos.

Even though I already have hundreds of case studies and rave reviews, why do I continue to collect this sort of stuff? Simple. It's the proof - the authority assets - that demonstrate beyond a shadow of a doubt that I'm the real deal.

Rave reviews as we called them, recorded "in the wild" as it were, are the most natural sounding and they really help to cut through the layer of mistrust that consumers have developed in their attitude towards many marketing efforts.

This is so important that I would make it someone's job for the day, either one of your staff or the family member helping you out, to get every attendee to record a testimonial before they leave the workshop. If they're an existing customer, get them to talk about why they love your products and services. If they're a new customer, get them to talk about the workshop and what their biggest take-aways from the day were.

Just remember, some people are self-conscious about talking to a video camera, so make sure you have a space for them to do it where they can record some comments without everyone else in the room watching. Also, make sure your camera operator is prepared with two or three questions to ask the attendees. Some people will happily talk to a camera for five minutes about why they love your stuff, whereas others need a couple of questions to help them get started.

Here are a few questions for those who need help:

- Please introduce yourself and tell us where you're from.

- What were the biggest take-aways from today?

- What would you say to someone thinking of attending an event like this?

When the day comes, your head will be so full of the content you're delivering, making sure that everyone is comfortable and ensuring the video cameras are recording everything properly, it can be easy to think that testimonials are just one more thing to worry about and maybe you'll just skip this step for your first workshop.

Please, please don't.

Not recording video testimonials while you have happy customers in the room is so wasteful it should be illegal! Just keep in mind, if they took the trouble to attend your workshop, these are some of the happiest customers you have.

Along a similar line, I'd also suggest having someone whose sole job is to manage your social media accounts (setting up a hashtag for the day), posting photos, quotes and engaging those who couldn't attend your event. This paves the way for the promotions you'll be creating off the back of your workshop over the coming months.

This will also put you in good company - take a look at Richard Branson's social media accounts. He's really good at posting photo evidence of all the cool things he's doing in his life, in his business, in his charity work and so on. He's built this Branson brand that presents him as an epic, larger-than-life character.

You don't have to go to those lengths, but in the interest of documenting everything, posting photo proof of your event is a great way to set the ball rolling.

Remember, one of your overriding goals is to develop yourself and your business as an authority. Rave reviews and photos are a huge piece of the puzzle and are as crucial as anything else you accomplish at your first workshop.

Stick with it, you're on the right track and the rewards are worth it.

In my experience, the difference between those who make it happen and those who don't, is a willingness to throw your hat over the wall.

You know this story, right? Three guys are on a long journey that is interrupted by a huge wall, blocking their path, seemingly too insurmountable to allow them to continue. Then one of the guys takes his hat off and throws it over the wall, saying "well, now we've got no choice but to find a way over."

If you throw your hat over the wall, in this case, by setting and announcing a date for your workshop, you'll find a way to make it happen. Once you've completed your first event, there'll be no doubt in your mind that you've completed the most challenging element of Authority Content and every step that follows is going to be easier and easier to execute.

Throughout the rest of this book you're going to see exactly why a workshop gives you everything you need to power your marketing, basically forever. At this stage of Authority Content you've presented your expertise. Now it's time to start creating your package.

Chapter 7 Exercise

Create a checklist for the day of the workshop. Include; bringing an itinerary, video release forms, testimonial questions, etc. Delegate responsibilities such as: checking in attendees, time keeping, managing your social media, collecting testimonials, taking photos etc.

Or if you own the Authority Content "Do It Yourself" course, download our completed checklist from the members' area.

08. PRODUCTISE YOUR AUTHORITY

Nice work, you've captured all this beautiful content, several hours of condensed expertise on video, ready to share with the world.

So what are you going to do with it?

You've probably already figured out that you're going to share portions of the content online as a means of promoting you and your business. In fact, if you've followed the previous chapter's suggestions, you've probably already leaked a few photos and video snippets.

However, before we get to the "Promote" stage, we need to work on the "Product" stage. Here we need to decide how and where you're going to share the content as a "complete package." Ultimately, we're going to package up the video recording of your workshop and display it as a valuable piece of digital training material. This can then be either sold, given as a bonus or given away.

If you've never created a digital information product, you might be wondering why I rave on about them. Well, for starters, should you decide to sell it, the delivery cost is virtually nil, providing you with a superb margin on every sale. But what I love most about information products is the variety of different ways they can be used.

They make perfect up-sells to add extra profit to every sale. You can cross-sell them when someone buys another related product. You can even use them as down-sells.

For example, here's one of the ways I use them. If we get SEO prospects who say they can't afford our "done for you" services, we suggest they get the cheaper "do it yourself" home-study digital product. In this way, I don't have to discount our services and yet I still have an option for those with smaller budgets.

Now, I know the idea of selling digital products won't work for everyone, so don't worry if selling a training video package sounds like a poor fit for your business. The selling part is optional. There are multitudes of ways you can use it. The main purpose of this stage is to put a value on your workshop content and make it stand out in the marketplace.

Everyone has information overload these days, so to cut through the general noise of the marketplace, your content needs to be valuable, relevant and important. It won't appear that way unless you package it up and position it correctly.

To be clear, I'm not saying you should take something of no value and pretend it has worth. Your workshop recordings absolutely have inherent value, because you put time and effort into producing them and the knowledge you share in these videos is important and useful to your target market. However people's perception of your product, before they purchase it, will be based at least in part, on what's included and how much you charge or value it.

So whether you decide to sell it for several hundred dollars or give it away as a bonus on top of other high-value purchases, in most cases I suggest you assign it a value. In a moment we can talk through some pricing options, but first you need to know what you're putting a price on.

Don't Edit Your Own Videos

Our "keep it simple" theme is going to continue here, but that isn't to say that you can just sell all of your video content in its raw state. You need to apply a little polish to enhance the value of the content you're giving to people.

Don't fall into the trap of thinking you can edit the content yourself. It's really easy to get pulled into this rabbit hole only to realise after a few weeks that it's going to take you months to get the raw content into shape. A professional editor, on the other hand, is going to get your video whipped into shape in a very short time frame, and this is crucial to ensuring you maintain momentum and begin utilising your content. Hopefully you have some profits left over from selling tickets to your workshop, but even if you don't, this is still a worthwhile investment.

Tell the editor that you want the footage to contain nothing but the core content. That is, chop out anything that wouldn't be relevant to someone watching it after the fact.

Your editor should also review the testimonials, tidy them up and turn each one into an individual video file – these will be perfect authority assets for your website!

The final job of the editor is to encode the video in a format that is suitable for streaming online. Burning the videos onto DVDs or copying to a USB drive and posting them to people is an option, but it adds additional layers of complexity that aren't really necessary. If you really like the idea of having a physical product to hand over to people, I suggest saving this for your second workshop so you don't end up getting bogged down in something that turns out to be more trouble than it's worth.

Adding Value To Your Product

The second part of your product creation is putting together a package and this means we're going to return to the concept of perceived value. The video on its own is valuable, but the more useful extras you can pile on top, the higher the perceived value.

It's the difference between buying your favourite movie on Blu-ray, or buying a "collectors edition" that also includes a second disc of behind-the-scenes footage, a music soundtrack, and a book of concept art. That's the feel that we're aiming for.

There are probably lots of additional elements you can include in your product if you engage in a little creative thinking. Here are a few of the typical extras I like to include:

Alternative Versions: Not everyone enjoys watching videos, so I also include the mp3s from the workshop as well as the transcripts for those who prefer reading.

I'll add a special note about the transcripts, since we'll use this later in our promotion stage. In short, once the videos are edited it's good to get those transcribed. I get my Mum to transcribe all of my personal projects and while she's not for hire, there are plenty of great transcription services available online.

Workbook: If you created a workbook for your workshop attendees, you can add this to the package in PDF format. Your viewers can print out the workbook and refer to it while watching the video.

Workshop Slides: The slide deck from each of the speakers with space for notes is also a nice extra to complete the package.

Gift Vouchers: This can be a great addition and a way to transition those looking to "do it themselves" into "done for you" clients. Often, once someone understands your process and can see the value you add, they'll be keen to work with you. Gift vouchers give them that extra incentive for them to take the next step.

Free Consult: If your product carries a high price tag, you could even include some one-on-one consultation time with yourself or one of your team. This creates added value for the customer and is also a great way of getting to know your customers. Use this opportunity to build a relationship and find out what their needs are and potentially identify areas where you could be of service.

How To Deliver Your Product

Your workshop is now edited together into a slick and consumable video. You've packaged up the video files along with a whole host of tasty extras. So, how are you going to deliver this to your customers?

Would you be surprised if I were to suggest, at least for your first attempt at an Authority Content campaign, that you keep things really simple?

No? Good. That means the message is sinking in.

I have already mentioned that digital delivery is going to present far fewer challenges than delivering your package on a physical DVD or flash stick, but even then I would encourage you not to get caught in the details.

Your web designer will be able to advise you on the best approach based on your existing website setup but something as simple as a payment button behind which is a password-protected page containing your download links is a good idea.

At the time of writing this book, a simple blog with a shopping cart plugin is more than sufficient for your needs.

It's not that I don't believe you're capable of producing something more impressive, it's just that, to be frank, the first time anyone works the Authority Content system, they always make a few blunders (and I'm including myself in that).

The mistakes don't actually matter that much. You can stumble multiple times and, as long as you follow the process, you'll still see some great results at the end. What I don't want to happen, is for you to get so bogged down in the details that you lose momentum and give up halfway.

This is why I keep saying to keep things simple, move through the process as quickly as you can and once you've completed one campaign, you can use the experience you've gained, as well as the additional profits, to do an even better job the second time around.

What Price To Sell For?

How are you going to position and price your workshop package?

If you already sell digital products, it might simply be an additional, highly valuable package to place in your store.

If you run a service-based business, it could still be sold as a stand-alone product, but you might find it makes more sense to offer it as a bonus to your new and existing customers.

For example, if you sell high-end home security systems and your workshop is about how to make your property more secure, you could give away the video as a bonus to everyone who makes a purchase. Or you could sell the video on your site for $99.

Or perhaps you own a web hosting business and your workshop is about how to use WordPress to build great websites. Again, you could sell the video on your site for $199 but offer it as a free bonus to every customer who upgrades to a dedicated server package.

As I mentioned earlier, selling digital products doesn't always fit. For example, one of the case studies at the end of the book is with a pool manufacturer and clearly, in that case, selling a $97 course on how to build a swimming pool wouldn't make sense. Instead we turned the content into an open resource "buyer's guide."

There's no "one size fits all" answer to how you should best use your new digital product, you just need to think about what makes sense for you. In practice, you're not going to know until you try it and measure the results. So don't worry about getting it perfect. Just pick an angle, see what happens and then adjust accordingly.

Digital product example:
www.authoritycontent.com/digitalproduct

Open resource example:
www.authoritycontent.com/openresource

Selling Your Product and Making Some Quick Cash

Selling your product, as I mentioned earlier, is optional, but if it makes sense and fits with your audience, it can be a great way to continue to profit from each stage of the Authority Content process. Even if you're not intending to carry out any particular promotions, consider completing one or two of the steps below, as some will feed into the success of the "Promote" phase.

Getting the Word Out

Step 1 – Ask for feedback: Send review (i.e. free) copies to your workshop attendees, event partners, and VIP clients, and invite them to send you feedback. Ask them to tell you what they liked, what they didn't like and if there's anything else you could add to make the package even better value.

If you're getting good feedback and if they haven't already done so, this is another opportunity for you to ask for testimonials. You may also identify potential promotion partners.

Step 2 – Email Your Database: Having made any adjustments based on the feedback phase in step 1, I approach step 2 in the same way as I promote the live workshops. I send a couple of teaser emails before making the sales page live, and I make sure to include an "early bird" offer to encourage people to take immediate action. The "early bird" offer doesn't necessarily have to be a discount on the price. It could also be an additional bonus, such as an exclusive webinar or gift voucher for your next live workshop.

Step 3 – Joint Ventures: Start with your close business colleagues and then move on to any people and/or businesses you partnered with during your workshop. Most will be happy to recommend your product to their audience, particularly if they've been involved and appear in the videos. These people already know your product is great and will be able to talk intelligently about it to their customers.

Step 4 – Cross Promotions: This final step takes a little more effort but can be very lucrative. The idea is to find companies that provide products and services that are complementary to your business, without being directly competitive. Invite them to review and, if they like the program, potentially give away your product as a bonus to something that they sell. You don't directly profit from this exercise but it's a superb way of widening your market reach and gaining access to their best clients.

All of this goes back to our earlier discussion about using workshops to demonstrate your expertise, to educate people on how to consume your product correctly and to create joint ventures with other people in your industry. Whereas your "live" workshop only reaches a roomful of people, the video recording of your workshop can reach hundreds or even thousands of clients and prospects.

This final step is starting to cross the line into the "Promote" stage, which is perfectly fine because we're now ready to move on to this final part of Authority Content.

Chapter 8 Exercise

- Do some research and get an idea of the cost involved to edit your workshop footage. Factor this into the price tag you put on your live workshop tickets or at the very least resolve to make this investment.

- Make a list of extras you plan to include in your package. Give particular thought to any bonuses or freebies you can include that will massively add to the perceived value, while also performing a marketing function for your business.

- Talk to your web designer about the best platform for delivering your product or get some bids on your favourite freelancer site for a simple sales page, payment button and download page design.

- Review all of the above four steps outlined above and plan out how you're going to approach each one. You don't have to complete every step but I recommend giving them consideration. This ensures when the time is right you're ready to move quickly.

---

09. ROCK SOLID FOUNDATIONS

The final "P" in the Authority Content Marketing system is "Promote" and often this is the section that most people are interested in.

Perhaps you already have a great product or service and all you're really interested in is some ideas on how to spread the word. Maybe you've even skimmed the previous chapters, eager to start the content syndication.

Well, to be fair, if you skipped most or all of the previous sections, I'd be very surprised if you hit a home run.

Like I said earlier, Authority Content is not a good system for those who are always looking for short cuts and loopholes. I can tell you how to speed up some of the stages, but you need to be committed to the process to see the kind of results that I've experienced and that many of my clients and students have been able to replicate.

Just as it's important to lay solid foundations before you start building your house, there's still a little bit more work that needs to be done before you can start crafting your syndication plan. We need to spend a little time preparing your website into the best possible shape.

One of the primary reasons for this is to ensure you get the maximum SEO benefit. Obviously we want the maximum traffic that can be gained and therefore some consideration of what Google wants is key. You see, SEO is a much broader subject than it ever used to be. How people engage on your site, how quickly it loads, whether it's mobile friendly or not, and so on, are all important factors now.

Now, I'm not going to attempt to give you a crash course on SEO in this book – I have plenty of other material available that covers this subject in depth – but the mind-set I want you to adopt is a holistic approach where everything connected to your website optimisation is inter-connected.

As with so much of Authority Content, these improvements and optimisations will only have a real effect if you get them all working together. If, for example, you get your links cleaned up but your website offers a poor user experience, your good work in the first instance won't yield a great result.

But get all aspects working in harmony – that's when the magic sets in. It has a kind of multiplier effect.

It's a little bit like in a Maths exam where you get 1 point for using the correct working out, 1 point for getting the right answer, but you get 3 points if you get both correct. It's ironic that the scoring system in a Maths exam is basically 1+1=3 but this is the kind of bonus you get when you tackle usability, technical integrity and links.

Why Aren't You Ranking?

This might help to explain why your website isn't currently ranking. As an SEO expert, I often get calls from frustrated business owners because they're being outranked by a competitor, even though they've worked really hard at generating lots of back links and they have got an older, more well-established site.

Upon closer inspection, nine times out of ten the problem is down to one or two specific optimisation points. And they usually fall under one of three categories:

- Usability

- Technicals

- Incoming Links

So, rather than waiting until you're butting heads with the competition or get hit with a Google algorithm update, it makes sense to address these three areas now. Furthermore, this gives your Authority Content the best chance of success. In all likelihood, none of these areas will present you with any massive issues and it'll simply be a case of tidying things up.

Let's do some diagnostic tests on your site and get it ready for battle!

10. IS YOUR WEBSITE USABLE?

Remember, Google's primary goal is to provide the best user experience and serve the best and most relevant content to its users. With this in mind, we need to ensure your website is aligned with Google's goal!

Your biggest asset in this area is going to be your web designer. Whether you handle this in-house or hire an external web designer, you need to be working with people who are up to date with modern best practice.

Your web designer needs to be on the same 'page' in that the primary objectives of your website are to engage visitors, make it easy for them to navigate from page to page and ensure it's easy for them to find what they're looking for. This goal of engaging your visitors, keeping them onsite for as long as possible and creating an excellent user experience trumps virtually every other priority.

The fact is, designing a great website is less about looking pretty (although that's important) and EVERYTHING to do with usability. So where do you start?

Below are the essentials that you need to get right. Think of these as the minimum requirements for getting a pass from Google.

Responsive: First and foremost your website must look great on all devices – mobile, tablet and desktop. With people accessing the internet on a variety of devices, your website needs to be able to adjust accordingly. The term used to describe this is "responsive design" and any good website developer should design following the "mobile first" mantra.

Quick loading: Tied to the "mobile first" mantra is the idea of quick loading. As more and more people use their phones to browse the Internet, optimising your site for mobile devices and keeping website loading times to a minimum has become crucial. Just think about it from your own experience; how frustrating is it when you click a result in Google only to have to wait 10-20 seconds for the page to load. Google now has this as a ranking factor.

Navigation: Easy and intuitive navigation is a must. You can measure how well you're doing with this by looking at your Google Analytics and seeing if any pages are getting relatively low clicks and views. A low click-through rate could mean the page is hard to find or badly labelled in your navigation or not useful. Either way it should be fixed.

Essential Pages: A respectable online business will, without fail, contain an "About Us" page, a "Contact Us" page and a "Privacy Policy" page. If you're missing any of these pages, even if they're combined in some way with other content, create them and have clear links to them from your homepage. People and Google expect to see these pages on a commercial website, so having these available will increase the trust visitors have in you and your website.

Photos and Videos: Adding visual content to your site not only makes it appear more appealing, it also increases the length of time that people stay there. People can skim-read an article in under a minute, but watching a five-minute video always takes five minutes. Fortunately, thanks to all the material you gathered in the "Present" stage of Authority Content, you have plenty of content available to add to your site.

Beyond The Basics

Of course these are just a few minimum requirements for a great website and the astute reader may be looking for some specific metrics to focus in on. If you haven't already done so, it's worth setting up Google Analytics and narrowing your focus in on user metrics like bounce rates, time spent on site and number of pages visited. By focusing on improving these numbers, you'll inevitably improve your site's usability.

For example, if the majority of people who click on your website in the Google rankings hit the "back" button (giving you a high bounce rate for that page), that's a sure sign that either your website is not relevant to the search term or simply that your website provides a poor user experience.

Conversely, if the average visitor spends at least five minutes on your website and the majority never return to Google, this indicates that you've helped Google achieve its goal of delivering a website that is relevant to the search term entered by the user.

By focusing on improving your user metrics, the steps you take will result in higher rankings.

Chapter 10 Exercise

Ensure your website displays the minimum five essentials featured in this chapter:

- o Responsive
- o Quick loading
- o Navigation
- o Essential pages
- o Photos and videos

Chat with your web designer about how else you can improve your website's usability.

---

11. GEEKY WEBSITE STUFF & TECHNICALS

When I talk about "technicals", I'm basically referring to the technical side of how search engines view your website – sitemaps, indexing issues, 404s and other errors. I know it might sound quite "technical" but it's not as difficult as it once was to debug these sorts of issues.

Since Google introduced the *Search Console*, a lot of the hard work has been removed from the process.

So, if you haven't already set this up, Google "Google search console", perform a couple of dances to reassure Google that you own the site that you're registering and you'll be gifted with access to a huge array of reports about your site.

Note: The information provided in the Search Console is different from the information you would get inside Google Analytics. In the Search Console you'll discover how Google views your site and how to optimise its performance in search results. The important thing to look for is anything that Google has flagged as an error or needing attention.

This is the closest you'll get to Google saying "do this, and we'll give you better search engine rankings," so if there's something they're not happy with, get on it right away.

Aside from problems with incoming links (more on this in the next chapter), the most common issues are related to duplicate content, indexing problems and dead internal links. These are really easy fixes – or at least they're easy for your web designer – so there's no reason why you shouldn't get these resolved.

Now, to avoid this section of the book getting too technical or bogged down in details, simply ask your web developer, webmaster or whoever is managing the site to review this chapter. Using the following checklist they should be able to quickly ensure the health of your site.

HTML improvements: Fix duplicate, short or missing titles, description and content.

Manual actions: Has Google taken any targeted action or applied a penalty to your site? If it has, work to have this lifted.

Mobile usability: Fix any issues identified with regards to the mobile readiness of your site.

Crawl errors: Fix any 404s and ensure Google hasn't identified any sitemap issues.

Of course there's always more to be fixed but these are the most important areas. Your goal is to get a clean bill of health from Google on the technical front, so that in its eyes, your website is considered strong and dependable.

Spammy On-Page SEO

You also need to review your on-page SEO – especially if you've had any SEO work done in the past. Gone are the days of selecting keywords and then jamming them into as many places on a page as you can.

Put the visitor first and write for them. While it goes without saying, I'll say it anyway, don't write garbage or low-quality content with the objective of optimising it for a keyword. Yes, a single primary keyword or phrase is still considered best practice.

However, I am very careful to match the right keyword to the right page and it's always written to a very high standard.

Start with the most important words, related to your business, if they're not currently being served on your site. Keywords related to your products, brand names and team members, for example, are a great place to start. In fact, if you're not #1 on Google for your brand name, this should be your top priority.

Then, using Google's auto suggest, related keywords and other keyword tools, you can build a keyword list of relevant words and phrases. Optimise existing content so each page is focused on a relevant keyword and follows these few simple rules about keyword optimisation:

- Choose one primary keyword per page.

- Put that keyword once (not more than twice) in the meta-title and meta-description.

- Put it in once in the title on the page itself and a few times in the body content or wherever it fits naturally.

Avoid formulas or set ways of optimising pages. Focus on what creates the best user experience and if you have to compromise between usability and SEO … always default to creating the best user experience.

Also, don't spend any time optimising non-content pages (such as your "Privacy Policy" page) for specific keywords because you don't actually want these to rank. If someone searches on one of your most relevant search terms and arrives on your "terms and conditions" page, clearly that provides a poor user experience and is likely to bounce people away.

***

With everything in this section, aiming for perfection is not realistic. Fixing as much as you can, as well as you can, is what the goal should be. Although Google is scoring you on every little detail, some issues are more important than others and the strength of the competition is also a significant factor.

My point is that if there is a particular area that needs addressing and you're aware that the time and cost required is going to be significant, you need to make a judgement call on whether to get stuck in or whether to leave it for later.

If you're already ranking okay and the element you're considering doesn't appear to be harming your success, focus on the quick wins first and you can come back to the more difficult problems later. You just need to stay one step ahead of your competitors. You don't need to be perfect in the eyes of Google.

Chapter 11 Exercise

Review Google's *Search Console* service, fix any outstanding issues and then review your on-page optimisation. Avoid any sneaky or spammy techniques that aim to game Google. Things like doorway pages, sneaky redirects, content spam, keyword stuffing, etc are all doing you more harm than good. It's time to level up your game.

Don't worry if this spins out into a couple of weeks' work. It's important to your overall results and is time well spent.

12. QUICK WIN INCOMING LINKS

With your usability and technicals all attended to, the third and final spoke in our website wheel is your incoming links.

Syndicating and sharing content – which is what we're going to get into in the next chapter – will generate plenty of new links, but once again, there's some preparatory work you need to put in place first.

In SEO circles, we used to talk about each incoming link representing a vote for your website and being the be all and end all of ranking. To a certain extent they're still extremely important, but it's been a very long time since merely getting more votes than the competition is enough to outrank them.

What's required is to have your links "count" changed. Quality, diversity and relevance must now be the backbone of your link generation efforts.

Which of course, brings us back to the concept of creating links that serve the user above all else. You can still find places that offer to create hundreds of incoming links to your site for $5, but do you really believe that anyone's getting any love from Google for that kind of practice?

The irony is that if SEO practitioners had always practiced quality, diversity and relevance in their link generation efforts, they could have maintained great search engine rankings consistently, through pretty much every Google update, without ever having to make any significant changes to their strategy.

There's really no need to overthink this or get bogged down in the minute details of link anchor text, IP ranges and the velocity at which you build links. All you need to focus on is putting great content on relevant sites, spreading your efforts across a relatively broad range of locations and linking back to something relevant on your site.

Weed Out Problem Links

So, have you had any SEO work done on your site in the past? Before creating anything new, it's sensible to review your existing links and attempt to remove any that could be flagged by Google as manipulative or spam.

If Google has already found something along these lines, you may have seen a notification in your Search Console account. As noted earlier, if you've received one of these, follow it up without delay and then take whatever action has been prescribed and follow through with a reconsideration request.

While it used to be possible to just drown out low quality, spammy links by generating a healthy volume of quality links, that's no longer the case. Until you resolve the issue, your other rankings will suffer.

Note: Unfortunately, if you had great rankings before receiving a Google penalty, fixing the problem won't instantly catapult you back up to the top. Chances are, that at least in part, your high ranking was a result of the "bad" links and your position was artificially inflated. Therefore, you'll be returned to where Google believes you should have been ranking in the first place.

Don't worry though, the Authority Content process will help you get back to where you were, but you need to be patient. Remember, this isn't some push button solution.

I would also recommend, even if you don't have any Google warnings, that it's a good idea to be proactive. Google suggests webmasters review their link profile from within the Search Console and look for low quality links. Site-wide links[1], particularly from a low quality site, are a problem waiting to happen and it's worth addressing them now, rather than having to deal with them later as part of a reconsideration request.

In fact, if you've been building links for a while – months or even years – it could be worthwhile hiring a reputable SEO firm to perform a link audit and help you identify any parts of your link profile that are either hurting you or are likely to do so in the future.

Once you're satisfied that your link profile is at least relatively clean, you can move on to creating some good quality links.

The Authority Content process will generate plenty of these good quality links over a period of months, but there are some quick wins worth getting. This is particularly valuable if your site is new and isn't really on Google's radar yet. You may already have some of these in place, so just work your way through and action any that are not.

---

[1] A "site-wide link" is a link that appears on every page of an individual site, other than your own.

Foundational Backlink Building

When thinking about backlink generation, start by thinking about your website.

Imagine your website's homepage at the top, below that the main pages – which are usually one-click away from the homepage – and then below that, the deeper pages which might be product pages, your blog or other pages like that.

Next, identify all the pages that would be suitable landing pages for your visitors. In other words, if an individual page is the first thing a visitor sees on your site, would it make a good point from which they could start working their way through your site and learning about your products and services?

If the answer is "yes", add this page to your list.

Now, when you have the opportunity to create a backlink, don't automatically point it at your homepage, first look to see if there's a more relevant page on your list that you can use instead.

As always, think user first and link second. The link description and the destination page should be relevant and interesting and not just thrown onto a random page for the sake of it.

Don't obsess over anchor text when creating your links. That is, the words you use to link back to your website. Google isn't as interested in this as it used to be and will know if you're trying to create a volume of links all containing the same or very similar anchor text for the purposes of ranking. Use relevant keywords in your link, when you have the opportunity, but otherwise a brand term or simply your web address is fine.

Now, armed with your list of suitable backlink locations, let's get you some easy wins.

Existing Contacts: Contact everyone in your business network, whether they're a top-level client, an authority who attended your workshop, a supplier, distributor or anyone else connected to your business and ask them if they'd be willing to place a link on their website. It could be on a "Partners" page, a "Testimonials" page, a "Recommended Suppliers" page, or even at the end of a guest article.

Local (relevant) directories: Yes, directories are still important and will be for a long time to come! That doesn't mean you should sign up to some mass auto-submission tool that posts your sites to thousands of junkie, low quality directory sites. Identify the directories that are relevant to your industry and local area. Manually sign up to those and take the time to fill out the details correctly and in full. Directories such as Yelp or Yellow Pages (TrueLocal if you're based in Australia) are good examples of sites in which you should feature.

Review Sites: This will be more relevant to some industries than others, for example – travel and restaurants, for example – but if a review site for your sector exists, try to tap into this, because it is essentially a link and testimonial opportunity, all rolled into one.

Register your business on appropriate review sites, and then as part of your process, chat with customers after they've purchased and invite them to post a review. Offering incentives to do this is fine as long as it's clear that it's NOT dependent on them leaving a positive review. Encourage honesty and welcome the occasional negative comment as an opportunity to improve your products or services.

Social Media: Aim to operate a minimum of two or three social platforms. These will become part of your content syndication. Facebook, Twitter, Google+ and maybe LinkedIn are the obvious candidates, but you should also consider platforms that are relevant to your industry. For example, is your target market on Instagram, Pinterest or even Snapchat? Go where your target market is and don't just join a platform because it's the current hot topic especially if you can't maintain it!

Chapter 12 Exercise

Start by auditing your link profile, especially if you've been generating links for a while, and clean up any spammy or dubious links. Next go for your easy wins, including network contacts, quality directories, review sites and social media.

---

13. TURNING ONE VIDEO INTO DOZENS

If you've fully applied everything we've discussed so far, not only are you ready to maximise the benefits of the promotional stage of Authority Content, but you should also be able to fully appreciate why the steps described in the next few chapters are so powerful.

You'll be able to see with absolute clarity how these remaining pieces complete the puzzle and provide your business with a strategy that is organised, powerful, flexible and easy to repeat again and again, as often as you need.

It probably won't surprise you in the least to learn that we're going to start with some video marketing. Before we begin however, I want to take a moment to talk about video. You've already read about how invaluable it was with the *Metastock* project and you've probably already gathered that it's fundamental to my current business projects.

I said that Authority Content isn't just a fancy term for YouTube marketing and I think I've proven that already, but that doesn't mean that video isn't going to play a crucial part in this strategy. It's just that YouTube is only one part of a larger strategy.

I mention this before we begin, because I need you to get on-board and accept how crucial this is to your marketing efforts. Video has been important for some years now and this trend shows no sign of slowing down.

Yes, new technology may come along that makes online video look better, run faster, and even become more interactive but it will still, at the heart of it, be video content that provides people with quick and easy visual access to the information they need.

Perhaps you're already sold on this idea. Maybe you've already embraced video as a necessary element of your marketing efforts but if you haven't, you need to change your view quickly. If you're not using video in your marketing, I feel you're being negligent in the promotion of your business. It will give you a clear competitive advantage.

I frequently experience occasions where I'm speaking to potential customers on the phone and they say that they feel like they already know me because they've been watching many of my videos over a period of weeks or even months. Can you even begin to appreciate how powerful that is? A potential customer, whom I've only just met, feels like they already know me. Do you recognise the level of trust that has already been created BEFORE I've ever personally spoken to that person?

No amount of articles and blog posts are going to be able to create that effect. It's just not going to happen without utilising video.

Video is also going to be a huge time-saver for you. It's the best way I know to be able to duplicate yourself. You record it once and yet it may be seen by hundreds, sometimes thousands or many hundreds of thousands of people.

My point is, that video is important and you need to embrace it and make it a crucial part of your marketing strategy. Sure your video efforts will start by repurposing some of your content from the workshop but I hope they extend well beyond that. Step out of your comfort zone and reap the rewards.

Time-Coding Your Workshop Video

At this stage, you've already got hours and hours of video that you recorded at your workshop. Now you're going to chop it up and turn it into 30-40 individual videos, maybe more, each between three minutes and ten minutes in length.

This is a job you can do yourself, but it's far better to assign it to members of staff. They don't need to have any video editing skills because all they're going to do is watch the footage and make time notations where a snippet should begin and end. It's also a good idea to have someone write relevant titles and descriptions for each video, and if possible, identify a keyword or phrase that relates to the video.

I call this process "time-coding a workshop". We set up a spreadsheet before watching the video to log everything. A note is made of the start and finish times, to the exact second, of each segment of video that feels like it could stand alone as a short video.

There's a bit of a knack to this process and you'll get better at it over time. But the idea is to identify portions of your workshop that when viewed in isolation, still make sense and teach at least one useful point. A way to test this is to imagine watching the video as if you know nothing about your business. If the video feels like it imparts something valuable, whether it's a small useful tip, or a major, potentially life-changing philosophy, then it's a good snippet.

Sometimes the snippet will be complete, with a beginning, middle and end. Sometimes it'll end on a cliff-hanger and we'll add a slide that says something like, "For more information, visit www..." That said, don't overdo the cliff-hangers because you want your content to build you a reputation as being generous and knowledgeable. Of course, there's nothing wrong with holding back the occasional nugget that's only available if someone buys the whole course but aim for a healthy balance.

The goal here is to set up all these doorways scattered on YouTube, each attracting people to them with the value of the content and then encouraging them to visit your site to learn more about your products and services.

And yes, you're going to put up virtually your entire workshop online, in short chunks.

That might sound odd, as if it's somehow going to devalue the video product you created, but this is the way I've always done it. In all those years, I've only ever had one person query it and in that instance I just refunded the guy.

Sure, there may be some people who trawl through your YouTube channel, spend hours working out the correct order and watching every single video online (and that's okay), but the vast majority of people are happy to pay a fair price to have the whole workshop in order, in one place, with your additional bonuses.

Remember, the workshop video project is only a part of the overall strategy that is designed to "sell" the benefits of the products and services you provide and demonstrate that you and your brand are the knowledgeable "go-to guys" for your industry.

So share your best content for free and you'll be amazed at the Return on Investment (ROI).

Delivering Your Video Content

Once you've finished the spreadsheet, hand it over to your video editor as a guide to chopping up the content into individual video clips. You should also arrange for her to add an intro and outro[1] graphic (or they can create one) that makes your work easily identifiable to the viewer and closes with a "call to action", usually to visit your website.

Once your editor has finished, you should have 30-40 videos ready to go. Next, load them onto YouTube but mark them as "private" so they're not available to the public. Use the title and descriptions created during the "time-coding" process to complete the profile for each video and think carefully about the action you want the viewer to take after they've viewed your video. The aim of the game is to get viewers onto your website where you can start to build a more developed relationship with them.

Always, always, always put your user first. While linking back to your site and creating engagement, your message needs to be

---

[1] An animated graphic that sits at the beginning or end of a video is referred to variously as an "intro", an "outro" or a "stinger". It usually includes your logo or brand image and lasts no more than 4-5 seconds.

helpful and never aggressive or spammy. The same holds true for the titles and descriptions you enter. Even though you've created these in advance, you should still take the time to review them in the context of the YouTube page once the video is uploaded. Keyword optimisation should be done carefully and never at the expense of creating something intelligible and interesting.

Similar rules apply from what we talked about earlier with regards to keyword selection and optimisation.

- Choose one primary keyword per content piece.

- Put that keyword once (not more than twice) in the title and description.

- Avoid formulas or set ways of optimising pages. Focus on what creates the best user experience. Stuffing an irrelevant keyword in the title for the sake of it, or cramming the same keyword over and over again in a description isn't going to help anyone.

When all the upload and description work is completed, you can start releasing videos (changing their status from "private" to "public") at a rate of, say, two or three per week, depending on how many videos you've managed to generate from the process. The goal is to have a three to six month period where every week, you have something new and interesting to share.

Great examples of this style of content can be found on our YouTube channel:

www.authoritycontent.com/youtube

Repurposing Your Video Content

This is where the magic of repurposing starts to happen by turning these videos into fresh, unique blog posts. The best bit is, since you'll be repurposing your original high-quality content, the standard stays high! This solves the problem many business owners face when working with freelancers to create content for their business.

Most freelancers either don't know the subject matter well enough to write about it confidently, or they'll charge like a wounded bull.

By repurposing your video content, you can hire people to help populate your blog simply by using transcripts of your videos[2] and posting them as articles on your blog with the videos above them. This is a really simple process that anyone in your business can do.

Each time a video is set to "public" on YouTube, embed the video into a new post on your blog, and below the video, paste in the transcript. The transcript won't appear anywhere else, so it won't be seen as duplicate content, and embedding the video on your site helps it to rank better on YouTube. Like everything, you SEO it and, of course, once the blog post is "live" you can share this article on your social media platforms.

Now that's how you create a rock solid post without spending hours making it perfect. It's great for your visitors and great for Google.

Curious to know what this sort of post looks like? Visit:

www.authoritycontent.com/blog-post-example

---

[2] There are loads of transcript services out there from as little as $1 per minute of video or audio. Just Google it.

Going Social

Each time you set a video to "public" and you create the blog post, you can share them on the social media accounts. Keep in mind that, depending on the social media platform you're using, it's always the best idea to customise the content to suit that platform. This sounds obvious but many people are still creating one piece of content and trying to syndicate it across all their social media in the same format.

In the case of Twitter, for example, remember that it's like a cocktail party where people are talking about interesting and helpful things they've spotted. So, linking directly to the video with a punchy headline would work well here.

Facebook is more about socialising and many use it to catch up with friends. You could upload the video directly to your Facebook business fan page (it's always best to have content appear natively on a platform) and I would suggest you don't make it appear too "salesy". The gentle, helpful approach works well here. Let the content do the pre-selling.

For LinkedIn, people tend to love the written word, so you have the option of either posting a link to your new blog post or even create the blog post right there inside LinkedIn's blogging platform.

Instagram is more of a photo-sharing site, so your videos might not be the best fit but perhaps you have some photos from the workshop you could share? Or maybe you can convert some of your best ideas, content or processes from the videos into infographics and post those?

So, be selective and even creative with your social media activity - mix it up a bit.

Although we mentioned this earlier, it's worth repeating that when platforms allow you to specify the anchor text in your links, don't get carried away and attempt to re-use the same three or four keyword phrases over and over again. Throw in some good keywords occasionally, but your brand name or simply the web address will suffice most of the time. Google has become a lot smarter about how it ranks webpages for different phrases and understanding what a page is actually about.

Once you get up to a certain level of authority in Google's eyes, it will start to take your onpage optimisation at face value and trust that your title and descriptions are representative of the content.

You want your content and SEO to be natural and the best advice I can give you in this area is not to overthink it. If you avoid over optimising you'll find that in time, everything starts to fall into place.

When it comes to your social media content, what you're shooting for is a scenario whereby, if someone were to visit all of your social media platforms on the same day, the theme and branding would be consistent, but the latest and recent content would be a little different.

Can you see how easy this is?

From a single workshop we've generated a premium video product to sell, 30-40 videos to post on YouTube, the same number of transcripts to add to your blogs and that's not to mention everything you can share on your social media.

There will be no "churning out" content at any point. Everything will be carefully selected, polished and optimised.

That doesn't mean each piece of your content has to be a multi-media extravaganza. It simply means that there needs to be thought and purpose behind everything you create and syndicate.

This syndication of your content is the key to maximising the benefits of everything you've created… and we're only just getting started.

Chapter 13 Exercise

- "Time-code" your video to identify 30-40 video snippets and write suitable titles and descriptions.

- Pass the data to your video editor to create the individual video files and add a nice intro and outro to each one.

- Upload the videos to YouTube in "private" mode. Review the titles and descriptions to ensure they're optimised, user-friendly and feature a suitable "call to action".

- Set the videos to "public" at a rate that ensures you have fresh content, every week for a three to six month period.

- Obtain transcripts of the videos and post them on your blog under the embedded video. Remember to apply best SEO practice here.

- Share the videos on social media as they go "live", mixing up the content and descriptions for different social media platforms.

- One final point: apart from giving personal attention to the title and descriptions for each video to ensure they're not overly optimised and have the right message-to-market match, the majority of this section can be delegated to one of your team.

If you're a one-person business, this is a good time to consider hiring an assistant or an outsourcing company to handle the regular weekly tasks of setting the videos to "public", getting the transcripts, posting to your blog and sharing via social media.

---

14. CONTENT REPURPOSING

Do you know the story of the hunting tribes who when they kill an animal use every part – the meat, the bones, the skin? They waste nothing and, in doing so, maximise the benefits from the hard work they put in to tracking and catching the animal.

Authority Content is just like that, except with less gore and a much smaller chance of being eaten by a lion.

After all the effort you've put into preparing and hosting a workshop, you've extended the benefits of that work for a further three to six months by turning the workshop into videos, photos, articles, and social media content.

That in itself would be impressive, but there's no reason you have to stop there.

You can continue to repurpose this content to create amazing additional content that will attract people to your website and your business. How?

Here are five more ideas to give you a hint of what I mean.

Guest Posts

Hang on, didn't Google say guest blogging as an SEO strategy is dead? It's funny how often I hear this and it's not just limited to guest posts. At some point just about all strategies have been deemed "dead". So, what gives?

Well, it's not so much the strategy that's dead here, it's the way in which you do it. Yes, creating spammy, low-quality articles and posting them on blog networks that were created for the sole purpose of building backlinks is dead but...

If CNN.com came to me and asked me to comment on an area where I'm considered an expert, I'm not going to say, "No thanks, guest blogging is dead." Great high quality content, placed on quality sites that your audience visits, will never die as a strategy!

So, we've already created blog posts that are essentially a video with the accompanying transcripts of the video. The next level in this process is to spin the transcript into a stand-alone article.

By "spin", I don't mean passing the transcript through article-spinning software and creating a nonsensical collection of words that no one will want to read. I mean hire a writer to produce a well-crafted article that is based on the content in the transcript.

In fact, a skilful writer will probably be able to produce multiple articles from a single video transcript.

Although the teaching points may be the same as those contained in the video and the transcript, the content is most definitely unique and can be used on your blog, on social media sites and especially in guest-posting opportunities.

Find high-profile bloggers in your space, with a strong readership, who rarely post guest articles and try to come to some kind of arrangement. This step is even easier if you begin with the experts and businesses that contributed or partnered with you at your workshop.

You can get buy-in for this approach if you create articles based on the content that the experts themselves delivered at your event and invite them to use the article in their own name. As long as the guest post references your event and includes a backlink somewhere, everybody wins.

Press Releases

Yes, I know, I know... press releases are dead! Well, that's true if we're talking about spamming out press releases to the four corners of the Web through delivery services that do little more than clog up the email inboxes of journalists. But we can still use a couple of services and get great results. Like everything these days, the secret is putting out great quality content.

There's the dual benefit of both SEO and more importantly, building long-term contact lists of industry-relevant journalists. Almost every industry has its own print and online magazines and the journalists who work for them are almost always crying out for help in finding new, interesting and relevant stories.

Many of these sites will have some kind of onsite press release submission service, but it always helps if you can take the time to talk to and get to the know the journalists personally, either by telephone or by arranging a meeting at an industry event. You can even invite them to cover your future events.

Finding newsworthy topics about which you can write a press release is one of the key challenges, so one of the techniques I like to use is to identify the videos in my YouTube channel that are getting higher than average views and write a release that highlights its success or the ideas that are covered there.

Even if the release doesn't get any major traction but does find its way into news items somewhere online, this can result in a handy boost for the popularity of the video.

Again, be selective. With this approach one or two press releases every few months is plenty and forces you to focus only on your most popular and potentially-newsworthy content.

Check out our preferred press release provider here:

www.authoritycontent.com/pressrelease

Infographics

Infographics, if you're not familiar with them, are large images (usually long and narrow so they fit nicely into a blog post) that are made up of a series of interesting facts, and often statistics, and presented in a visually interesting way.

Faster to read than an article and frequently more memorable, the best ones get shared again and again on social media and blogs.

Not every video you produce will translate well into an infographic, so be selective. Take a handful of your biggest and most important ideas and tips, organise them into a simple list or chart, and then hire a top-notch graphic designer to create something beautiful.

Check out one of our favourite infographic sharing sites:

www.authoritycontent.com/infographics

Slide Sharing

Slide Share sites are a popular way to share slide decks from PowerPoint or Keynote style presentations. They sit comfortably in the middle ground between the visual appeal of videos and the speed of accessibility provided by written content.

You already have the slides that you created for your workshop, so it's simply a case of chopping them up into portions (in a similar fashion to time-coding the video) and perhaps adding some additional explanatory text.

Check out one of our slide sharing sites:

www.authoritycontent.com/slideshare

Podcasts

How about this for another idea? Video files are very easy to turn into audio files. From that point, there's nothing to stop you putting them online, in sequence, as a podcast. You'll need to chop up the workshop video a little differently – using larger chunks, and keeping everything in logical order – but this is a great way to reach a very large and potentially new audience.

Since the podcast will contain, in all likelihood, the bulk of your workshop content, you may want to wait until your content has aged a bit so it doesn't interfere with, for example, your YouTube campaigns and any product sales you have going on.

Curious to see what one of these podcasts look like?

www.authoritycontent.com/podcast-example

Insert Your Ideas Here

What do all of the ideas in this list have in common, aside from the fact that I've been able to use all of these approaches to great effect? The answer is that I came up with ideas simply by visiting a site that permits user-generated content and adapting my workshop video content into a new format that is suitable for the platform.

It's not exactly rocket science[1].

Tailor your content to the platform and link back to either your site, a relevant YouTube video or one of your social media pages.

Back in the day, SEO practitioners used to obsess over things like "feeder sites" and separating different linking sites into specific hubs, but there's really no longer any need for that. We actually want Google to know that all of our content is linked together, that we're creating tons of great material and that people are

---

[1] Unless your business is, in fact, in the rocket science industry, in which case it's not exactly brain surgery.

loving and interacting with our videos, articles, social media pages, infographics, slideshows and everything else we're putting out there.

The only rule for this ever-increasing range of content we're distributing, one that has never changed, is that ultimately the content should always lead people back to the main site. Each piece of content should be part of a breadcrumb trail that, if followed, will eventually bring people to the cake – your website.

A Little Bit Of Quality, A Little Bit Of Patience

I hope you got the message earlier. When someone calls out that a strategy is dead, what this person usually means, is that spamming this technique to create backlinks and generate better search engine rankings is no longer working. This is usually because Google has tweaked its algorithm to stop people taking advantage of a loophole that results in a glut of poor quality content.

But if your content is good quality, posted manually with accurate titles and descriptions, in a location that is visited by real people – all of which should be true if you're following the Authority Content system properly – there's no reason why it shouldn't still work for you.

Even if its ability to improve your search engine rankings has reduced, as long as it's helping potential customers learn more about you and your business and find their way to your site, there's no reason why you shouldn't keep going.

So, simply find social media sites, content sharing sites and other industry blogs that are currently popular – or growing in popularity – and create content that is tailored specifically for that venue. Keep spinning that workshop content into an ever-growing arsenal of great content.

Also, a word to set realistic expectations here… not every piece of content you share will go viral. Some of that content will generate no interest, some will generate a little interest and some will generate a lot of interest.

The secret is consistency and every now and again, you'll hit a home run with a single video, article, infographic and it will generate tens of thousands of views.

Keep producing content in a consistent and considered fashion, keep SEOing it like you would any bit of content on your site and you'll do just fine.

Double Down On The Winners With Paid Amplification

When you do hit a home run, remember to make the most of it! As I said, occasionally you'll have a piece of content that gets x5, x10 or even x100 the amount of views and engagement as everything else. Often it's hard to know exactly why… maybe you hit a sweet spot with the subject matter, maybe you selected a great keyword or maybe an influencer shared it? Most likely it'll be a combination of a whole range of factors.

So, what do you do now to get the maximum exposure? A great strategy is to further amplify its success through paid channels. Depending on the type of content, you will have a variety of options. For example, a YouTube video can be promoted through with pre-roll advertisements. Images can be advertised through Pinterest's promoted pins. Guest posts, and/or your own blog posts, can be boosted through Facebook's ad manager.

There are many options and my goal is to not to list every possibility but rather get you in the right mind-set. The strategy of creating content and promoting your best bits through paid channels works a treat – and to take it one step further, you can then build remarketing[2] lists from this audience for future promotions.

This is starting to get exciting!

Chapter 14 Exercise

Continue to look for new ways to convert your workshop video content into new formats and once you've found a good source, add it to your own content syndication plan.

At the very least, make sure you explore the five alternative methods I share: guest posts, press releases, infographics, slide sharing and podcasts.

---

[2] Remarketing is a method of advertising to those who have visited your website or viewed your content. Previous visitors or users can see your ads as they browse the internet through the Google Display Network, YouTube, Facebook and other channels that offer this service.

15. REMEMBER YOUR EXISTING CUSTOMERS

Many business owners have been quoted as saying: "If I lost everything in my business overnight and I could only keep one thing, it would be my customer database."

That's true, because if you've still got your database of customers, you can send them new offers and rebuild your business pretty quickly.

If you're nodding your head in agreement, now ask yourself whether you might be guilty of taking your customer database for granted. Do you give your existing and previous customers the same level of time and attention that you give to your new leads? Do you email them on a regular basis, say, every week, month or even quarter?

If you do email them regularly, how often do you send them information on anything other than your latest special offer or product launch?

This is an important point. You know that your customer list is important and you know that it's easier to sell to an existing customer than it is to generate a new one, but what do you do in terms of making them feel valued and show them the value in your brand?

It's a little bit like when a guy starts a new relationship with a girl and showers her with time, attention, gifts, flowers and so on. But later on, once they've been together for a while, his attention starts to wane. How long is it going to be before she starts to feel unappreciated and starts drawing away?

The valuable, free content that you used to attract your customers in the first place, should still find its way to their inboxes after they become clients. No-one's saying you shouldn't send promotional emails on a regular basis, but it should be interspersed with emails that contain great content as opposed to yet another sales pitch.

The good news is that all the content you're creating as part of the Authority Content strategy can be used just as well to maintain your relationship with your existing customers as it can to attract new ones.

The trick to making this work is to be selective.

Every time you produce a new piece of content, you share it via social media and make sure that people know it's out there but your customer database should only receive the best of items, otherwise they'll soon start to get fed up or feel overwhelmed by the volume of material they're receiving.

All you have to do is let the Internet tell you which pieces of content are the most valuable, based on the number of views, shares and comments. If after a couple of weeks, a video you posted on YouTube is getting some decent traction, this is a good choice to email to your customers.

You can direct them to your blog where the video is embedded or send them a direct YouTube link. Either way, make sure you share the popular videos with your customers within 30 days of the video going live. There's evidence to suggest that the number of views received during the first month of publication has an impact on its ranking in the YouTube search engine.

Yes, that's right, this is a two-way street.

Your customers get great, free content, reminding them what a great source of expertise you are, and your most popular content gets a fresh spike of traffic, further impressing Google with its popularity.

Bang! Another benefit from the Authority Content!

Chapter 15 Exercise

Send weekly, monthly or bi-monthly emails to your customers informing them of your best and most recent free content.

16. WRITE YOUR OWN BOOK

Take a moment and go to the Amazon website, search the names of any well-known, successful business people you can think of and see if you can find one who HASN'T, at some point in their career, written a book or had a book written about them.

You'll struggle.

Virtually every businessperson of note has either become successful by writing a book or has capitalised on their success by writing a book. Why? Because it's a universally recognised way of identifying someone as an expert in a particular field.

It's even entered the English language as an expression. When we say that a person "wrote the book" on a particular subject, we're basically saying that this person knows more than just about anybody else about this topic.

Writing and publishing a book is the ultimate symbol of authority and can propel your expert position faster and with greater longevity than just about any marketing strategy. Even before you've read someone's book, the fact that it exists often elevates your view of that person.

There are lots of reasons this effect exists but I suspect a major factor is that people imagine – and quite rightly – that writing a book takes a lot of hard work and commitment. People imagine sitting at their laptop in front of a blank WORD document and wondering how they're going to put 30,000-80,000 words into some sort of logical structure someone else would want to read.

If the challenge of actually producing a book is the only thing stopping you, then think for a minute about how far you've come in terms of producing the content for a workshop and turning it into hours of video and thousands and thousands of words of transcripts and articles. How difficult would it be to take a transcript of your entire workshop and turn it into a book?

Okay, it's still pretty challenging and there's a hefty amount of work involved, but having completed your workshop, you're in a much better position than if you were going to write a book from scratch.

If for instance, you were to hire a ghost-writer to put your book together, you would normally have to spend hours and hours being interviewed to get all the information out of your head and into a format that the writer can work with. You'd also need to spend many more hours working out a theme and structure so everything comes together in a logical order.

By putting together the workshop, you've already done this work. Any ghost-writer worth her salt should be able to take a complete transcript of your workshop and produce a book that delivers your knowledge in your voice.

Of course, given the level of work required to write the book, there is a greater amount of expense involved than, for example, getting a writer to produce a few guest-posts. But the end result, in terms of the credibility that this book will add to you and your brand, makes this well worth your consideration.

Oh, and in case you're wondering if it's really feasible to turn a workshop transcript into a book...

You're holding the proof of concept in your hands.

Chapter 16 Exercise

This is the ultimate application of Authority Content. If you can find the funds to invest in the production of a book, based on your workshop, this will open doors of opportunity that you never even knew existed.

17. PLAY THE LONG GAME

Building a business is a marathon, not a sprint so... Warning! Shampoo marketing cliché alert!

That's right. Once you've completely exhausted every possible avenue of content creation from your workshop, simply rinse and repeat.

You could aim to run a workshop once every 12 months, slightly increasing the ambition of your production each time, but always using the results to power your marketing for the rest of the year. If you have the energy and the resources, you could even conduct your workshop twice per year.

Whatever schedule you decide upon, it's important that you repeat this process on a regular basis. Each time you do it you'll get a little bit better at the production, a little more fluid in creating content and you'll be building on the foundation of great content that you put out the last time.

This is how you Google-proof your business, turn on a flood of traffic, triple your conversions and establish long-term customer loyalty.

Every year that you're still around, still producing informative and valuable content, your status as an expert will continue to grow, your ability to attract new business will continue to improve, and your position in the industry will be unshakeable.

Create Your Own System

If I can give you one final piece of advice going forward, particularly on your second time through the Authority Content process, it would be to systemise and document the process as much as you possibly can. Outsource the "Product" and "Promote" phases or pass it down the line to members of your team who are capable of learning the process and managing it without needing you to handhold them.

We use a platform called www.systemHUB.com to organise and improve our checklists, processes and standard operating procedures (SOPs). This is critical because the systems within your business, outlining the way you do things, are the most valuable assets you own.

How about this for an idea: hire a marketing graduate to read this book, document and manage the entire project from start to finish. It could be the best $30,000 you ever spend. Or even better, for more established businesses, have my team implement the entire Authority Content process for you: www.authoritycontent.com/done-for-you

Long-term, this is the best strategy for you. SEO and online marketing is important work but it's not the best use of your time. Your involvement in the process should be creating and delivering an amazing workshop and then, after that, everything else should be handled by your team or outsourcers.

Stay On Target

Does Authority Content take a lot of time and effort to get off the ground?

Yes – although if you follow my advice to keep your first attempt as simple as possible, the rewards far outweigh the costs. Heck, deep down you know everything worthwhile takes time and effort.

Never lose sight of the goal we set out to achieve at the beginning of this book – to create a solution for growing AND marketing your business that isn't tied to the whims of whatever online platforms are currently popular.

Authority Content, by its very design, refreshes your marketing every year, without needing to massively overhaul your approach and without requiring you to nuke all your previous marketing assets.

***

It's pure hubris but I have this fantasy that you're actually reading this in the year 2100. The entire world is unimaginably different from how it was when I was alive, yet Authority Content, thanks to its ability to shape and adapt to its surroundings, is still powering businesses all around the world.

I sincerely hope that yours is one of them.

18. AUTHORITY CONTENT IN ACTION

Clearly one of my core philosophies is to be the best example of what I teach, so looking deep within all of my businesses you will find excellent applications of Authority Content. That said, I'm not the only one applying this strategy with great success. Here are small samplings of some of the businesses I've personally worked with to apply the process.

Case Study #1: Compass Pools Australia (CPA)

www.compasspools.com.au

Business: One of Australia's leading in-ground fibreglass swimming pool manufacturers.

CPA spent a day recording a series of videos in which team members spoke on a variety of topics. They invited a few members of staff and some guests to sit in and listen. The main goal of the day was to answer almost every question that a prospect might have before purchasing a swimming pool.

The videos were chopped up into 25+ videos and posted onto their website, along with transcripts, made accessible free of charge to any visitor. By creating a 'free to anyone' buyers guide, CPA was able to demonstrate their authority and build trust between the prospect and the business.

One of the side effects was a noticeably increased connection with their customers - probably because of the relaxed, conversational, friendly style in which the video content is delivered. Visitors to CPA's showroom have even recognised team members from the videos and, on a couple of occasions, have reacted as if they were meeting mini celebrities.

One CPA salesman even went to meet a prospect in their home and was greeted as if he was an old friend. It transpired that the customer had watched the salesman on video some weeks ago and was remembering the experience as if the salesman had previously visited him. This went a long way in selling a $50k+ swimming pool.

Some of the videos have been gaining great traction on YouTube with additional press releases used to amplify the results. The CPA team have been so thrilled with the results they're already planning their next round of Authority Content.

Watch the complete Compass Pools case study video here: www.authoritycontent.com/compass

Case Study #2: WP Elevation

www.wpelevation.com

Business: A business accelerator program for WordPress consultants.

WP Elevation ran a one-day "Master Class" event in the Melbourne CBD. Just over 30 people attended on the day and an additional handful of people who couldn't make it, purchased the option of receiving the recordings of the event. These sales alone allowed the event to break even.

After the event, WP Elevation used social media to talk about the Master Class and to promote the forthcoming sale of the edited version of the video recording. Approximately two months after the event, recorded material was placed on a membership site and access was made available during a limited window. Sales of access to the membership site generated $11,500 in just four days. The "Master Class" video package will now be used as a bonus product or as the subject of additional sales events.

At the time of writing, WP Elevation has only just started the "Promote" phase. However, based on its success so far, the owner of the business is expecting to see great results.

Case Study #3: Tradie Web Guys

www.tradiewebguys.com.au

Business: Helping tradies develop marketing solutions for their business.

Tradie Web Guys ran their first event with 30 people in attendance - each paid around $100 per ticket. Company founder, Matt Jones, arranged a number of different speakers and even lined up PayPal as a corporate sponsor. To keep his overheads low, he made an arrangement with a local video producer to film the event in exchange for some publicity. Additional coverage was obtained by contacting various technology sector publications and local television.

"I think if you've got a product and you know it can add value, you're not only cheating yourself but you're really cheating your industry by not getting it out there and doing some sort of Authority Content. It's about being present and getting guys together and the leverage that you can generate from that workshop."
– **Matt Jones (Founder), Tradie Web Guys**

Additional case studies can be found at www.authoritycontent.com

ABOUT THE AUTHOR

David's impressive journey begins as an author and coach to hundreds of day traders back in his early 20s. Perfecting his analytical eye from stock market trading, he was able to quickly see – and snap up – business opportunities all around him.

His business experience spans from one-off windfall projects (such as selling the Melbourne Cricket Ground - MCG), to developing and franchising retail stores, building a multi-million dollar portfolio of over 500 domains and websites, to turning his real world promotional skills into successful online marketing systems.

Some years on, David now focuses on his renowned SEO and web video companies: Melbourne SEO Services and Melbourne Video Productions. Together his companies help businesses grow through innovative online marketing systems.

Recognised as a high achieving entrepreneur and online marketer, David has been asked to keynote countless conferences and seminars including TEDx and Digital Marketing Summit Australia. He has been featured in dozens of publications, including *Australian Financial Review* and *Smart Investor* and also featured in other media such as Nova radio and Channel 9's *Today Show*.

David's fun and approachable personality, yet seriously impressive business background, ensures he relates to a wide variety of audiences – and keeps them on the edge of their seats with his captivating anecdotes. David's life is one of dedication, passion and the desire to learn; and those who seek the same triumphs are motivated by his story.

Companies & 'Done For You' Services

Considered by many as Australia's most trusted digital agency, Melbourne SEO & Video offers a wide range of services including: modern SEO, web design, web video and "Done For You" Authority Content implementation services. To find out how David and his team can help your business, book your complimentary business accelerator session here: www.authoritycontent.com/help

Or visit: www.melbourneSEOservices.com
and www.MelbourneVideoProduction.com.au

Authority Content - 'Done For You' Services

You're busy, you see the value of Authority Content and want my team to do it all for you.

By reading this, it's clear you're interested in building authority. In its simplest and purest form, Authority Content is precisely targeted marketing; consisting of a plethora of different media formats, that – when distributed – position you as the authority in your niche. This positioning becomes the undeniable and irrevocable proof that you are the "go-to" person in your industry.

When you create this type of high quality content, you'll effectively turn on a 'traffic machine', engaging both clients and prospects who are simply magnetised towards your expertise and waiting in line to do business with you.

With Authority Content 'Done For You', the team at Melbourne SEO & Video will take you through the three P's: Present, Product & Promote. We'll help you run the event, turn the captured footage into a product or resource guide and then promote it across the web.

It's the perfect program for busy business owners looking for the results without having to do the work. Curious to know exactly how it works? Watch the complete Compass Pools case study here: www.authoritycontent.com/compass

The next step

If you "get it" and can see the value in this strategy – the next step is for us to have a chat. It's an intensive program that gets amazing results – and that's what drives us – so we're very particular in choosing which businesses we work with. We want to be sure that we're a good fit.

To find out more and register your interest, visit: www.authoritycontent.com/done-for-you/

What have people been saying about Authority Content?

This book synthesises a body of knowledge, providing tangible tips for creating content that positions you and your brand ahead of the pack.
Rakhal Ebeli, chief executive officer of Newsmodo.com

I've been watching and applying Dave's Authority Content strategy for 8+ years... why? because it works! Built on rock solid principles, it's without doubt one of the most powerful and long lasting marketing strategies I have seen. It should be required reading for all business owners.
Pete Williams, co-founder of Infiniti Telecommunications

Ever since I first met Dave at a high level marketing conference back in 2008, I've been fascinated how he's able to deliver quality content in different formats across multiple channels, on a consistent basis. You'd expect him to look stressed and run off his feet, yet every time I catch up with him he looks relaxed and fresh. Now finally he reveals his secret sauce. He has the ability to appear in many places at once yet in reality he just has a very clever system that does the majority of the heavy lifting on autopilot. 'Authority Content' is a step by step guide to creating high value events for customers, clients & prospects. Then repurposing the content recorded at the event to produce a six month multi layered content machine that runs in the background, providing great value to your target audience whilst building your authority, even whilst you sleep. Clever!

Want to know where to start with your content marketing? This book is the template for you because Dave also has the ability to simplify and systemise the complex into manageable building blocks whilst showing you the short cuts to maximise your time & effort.
Kenny Goodman, founder of www.FindTheEdge.com

From one business owner to another; this is the only marketing book you need to read in this age.
Logan Merrick, director of Buzinga App Development.

David Jenyns is hands down my go to guy on Authority Content. When I was restructuring the content services at my digital agency I went through dozens of courses. David's book and training videos on Authority Content provided the leverage and time saving methods we were seeking.

David's techniques allowed us to produce all the content our clients required to become marketplace authorities with just one large investment of focused attention upfront as oppose to hours and hours of attention every single day. David is a master of using leverage and systems to produce high volumes of quality content that converts into attention, leads, customers and most importantly profits that just keep coming. I can't recommend 'Authority Content' highly enough.
Josh Denning, CEO of smartroi.com.au

If Dave is implementing it, you know it works and 'Authority Content' is a game changer.
Shane Price, director of StreamBiz

I speak to many business owners about franchising their business operations and am confident the invaluable information in this book will save them time, money and, importantly, lots of stress. It is intelligently written, well thought out, most constructive and unbelievably comprehensive.

I believe it should be required reading for every business owner who operates online, and will be of special value to those with multiple outlets.
Brian Keen, director of Franchise Simply

FINALLY: A repeatable process for establishing authority in an industry! By following David's advice, you'll transform yourself into an authority figure in your industry that attracts more customers and commands higher prices.
Eric Lancheres, founder of Lan Publications

This methodical book reveals the #1 way to attract new prospects and make your conversion rate soar – by establishing trust before talking to potential customers.

In the new world of 21st century marketing, social media and rapidly changing SEO rules, there may be no more important skill for long term success. Thankfully, Dave's outlined everything step-by-step.
Scott Bywater, founder of Copywriting That Sells

Gurus love to take concepts and hide them behind wacky practices and obscure terms so they can charge more - and keep you from being able to decipher the process. It's called "job security," or "trying to make the other guy look stupid."

David's book is the complete opposite of this practice - he spells it out, step by step, and with language and examples anyone can embrace and, more importantly, immediately implement. The power and process of Authority Content is yours to embrace, today ... and you'd be a fool not to do just that.

Paul Collegian, author of How to Podcast 2016 & YouTube Strategies 2016

David Jenyns is one of the sharpest marketer's around and 'Authority Content' is the proof. This extremely well thought out marketing system can't help but position you and your business as the authority within your industry. David's living proof of that - he's the best example of everything he teaches. Read every word and take action!

Gideon Shalwick, founder of veeroll.com

Are you awesome?

If you enjoyed this book, and think others might like it too, would you be so kind as to leave a nice review on Amazon.com? This helps to spread the word and with each 5 star review you post, you are making the world a better place :)

Just visit: www.authoritycontent.com/amazon

Thanks again, I appreciate your support and hope we get to meet some day.

Lightning Source UK Ltd.
Milton Keynes UK
UKOW02f2340190816

281114UK00005B/114/P